ENJOY THE APPLE: YOU PICKED IT

NANCY LEE BURNS

Nancy Lee Burns

Copyright © 2013

ISBN: 978-0-9886964-1-9

Published by
Nancy Lee Burns

Cover Design
Robert M. Lantry

Printed and Manufactured in the U.S.A.

Nancy Lee Burns

DEDICATION

To all Vietnam veterans—those living and those who have moved on.

"History is a combination of reality and lies. The reality of history becomes a lie. The unreality of the fable becomes the truth." Jean Cocteau, French author, director, poet (1889-1963).

.

CONTENTS

ACKNOWLEDGMENTS

Special Thanks to Carole Mathewson -
Editor Extraordinaire

1 PREFACE

*E*nergy swirls and, unseen to the naked eye, a shift occurs. Was it a dream? Her head nestled in her pillow, with eyes half open. It was a vivid moment, as full consciousness came to her. Something moved around her, and she felt energized. Was it energy generated by her? She felt an influx, like a jolt penetrate her body. Words, messages, floated in her consciousness like buoys on water. *"Choose wisely." "Choice stands, until a new choice." "Forgiveness precedes growth; lack of forgiveness stunts growth."*

Ann had always been interested in dreams, and during the previous month she had become more aware of being awakened by early-morning dreams. The dreams were about Eve and the Garden of Eden. They didn't frighten her. They were quite gentle. In her half-sleep state, she scribbled the words she remembered Eve had said to her in dreams. It was all recorded on her bedside pad of paper.

The apple is bright red, juicy and fragrant. It is tempting and impacts all the senses. If chosen, enjoy it, and find the God seed. Free will is about choosing God or not choosing God. That is the only choice ever. With that bite of apple,

I moved into separateness and enjoyed the taste. The separation led to expulsion. Finding the God seed led to resurrection and a return to the garden. Be willing to see the apple tree and the enticement of separateness without judgment, and choose God. If you eat the apple, find the God seed. Or skip the apple and go directly to God. Either way, it is your choice. Enjoy. It is quite simple.

My story isn't one of fear, judgment, redemption or punishment. It includes all, but it is a story about finding the gift of resurrection in all. In finding God everywhere, we reveal the Truth; we unmask the Presence. The crucifixions that occur now are the ones we do to our heart. Judgment and ego slow one down. Find and choose God first. Incarnation, followed by resurrection, is inherent in all creation. Go straight to resurrection.

Her alarm clock buzzed and brought her to full consciousness. She made her way into the kitchen. Her Monday morning began with the familiar smell of coffee brewing and chicken broth being poured over dog food for Chopper.

2 ANN AND BOB

*A*nn, a retired reporter who liked stories about whistle-blowers, enjoyed getting into the mind of the one who couldn't rest because he or she "had to know and tell the truth." Ann would say that whistle blowers were petting the elephant in the room, which no one wanted to see. History books were frequently rewritten because a detail was omitted or new facts had surfaced. In our judicial system, before DNA testing, one false witness sent many innocent people to prison for life. Ann frequently asked, "What is truth?" Her experience in crime reporting had taught her that most, if not all, criminals would let someone take the fall for them. The original fall guy, she had concluded, was Eve, who reportedly took the first bite of the apple in the Garden of Eden. Eve was the eternal scapegoat. How great if she, Ann, could have interviewed Eve. What if...? And thus began Ann's journey. She became infatuated with her perception of Eve.

A divorcee, Ann was spending her third summer in the small mountain community of Pine, Arizona. Pine, at an elevation of 5,500 feet, has a population of approximately 2,000. As temperatures reach 114 degrees in Phoenix, the great escape occurs, and lucky Phoenicians, who can, head for the mountains. The ponderosa pines are magnificent, and the area claims to be among those with the cleanest air on earth.

The Mogollon Rim stretches two-hundred miles, and the western end seems to embrace the Pine/Strawberry area.

Many describe the mountainous community as heaven on earth. It is the land of Zane Grey novels. The ponderosa pine forests of the Mogollon Rim are beautiful, but they are vulnerable to fire. The second-largest Arizona fire, the Rodeo- Chediski Fire, destroyed more than 450,000 acres in 2002. State wildfires in 2011 destroyed just over a million acres, and, in 2012, just under a quarter of a million acres.

A precious commodity, water is particularly sacred in times of drought. In previous summers, on certain days water in Pine was available only for cooking, bathing and drinking. Residents were prohibited from watering a garden and/or washing a car. Ann wondered how Eve obtained water after the fall. Their entire universe became new to Adam and Eve after the fall.

Ann continued washing dishes, her eyes closed. She was imagining what the Garden of Eden looked like before and after the fall. Did Eve, upon her expulsion from the garden, have a memory of it? Were the trees in the garden the same before the fall as after?

Ann's friend Bob knocked on the screen door, startling her into the present.

"Do you have coffee made? Where's Chopper?"

Ann unlocked the screen door and held it open for him.

"Come in, Bob. Help yourself." She pointed to the coffee pot. "Chopper is at the groomers."

Bob followed her into the kitchen. He knew where the mugs and sugar were, and he helped himself to java. Both moved to the deck.

He sat in his favorite place, a large wooden rocker. "What were you thinking, Ann? You appeared deep in thought. You didn't hear me walk on the deck." He took a sip and savored his view of Ann. To him, Ann was a fiercely independent woman with a chip on her shoulder. He had often wondered who or what had hurt her, and what made her ways seem so strong.

She interrupted his thoughts. "Is meditating thinking?"

"Don't get all Zen on me."

"You asked. Truthfully, I was contemplating the Garden of Eden. What did Adam and Eve see? What about all the animals? How did their fall from grace affect the animals?"

Bob gazed intently at her. "Where's this coming from? What's going on?"

"Just thinking about Eve. Imagine being in the garden and losing everything."

"Don't forget Adam. Without choice, he donated a rib."

"Makes me wonder if the female animals began with a rib from the male of the species. The Eve story is more interesting to me than the Adam story. Adam seems like a wuss."

"Male basher."

"And this is where you interrupted, or entered into my musings, Bob. I'm glad you did. Want a cookie?"

"No, thanks."

She got up to fill her cup.

Bob enjoyed his interactions with Ann. He found her intelligent, with a penchant for looking at things in a unique way. She made him think.

She returned with steaming coffee. "So, Bob, if Eve walked up the steps and sat on the deck with us, what would she say? Assuming she could speak, of course."

"Maybe they didn't need language in the garden? Ever thought about that?"

"What language did they create? Look at all the languages generated since that time."

"Assuming, Ann, that the Bible is even true, not everyone believes in it. I'll go along in this illusion, or delusion." He flashed a big smile at her. "In that instant of eating an apple their whole world changed. No way am I suggesting who ate it first, cuz I know what you will have to say."

Ann held her coffee cup in her hands. Bob had her full attention.

"It's like a before-and-after picture. The apple tree is the same." He motioned with his hands. "The snake and the sky were all the same. But the earth, as we know it, hung precariously in the great subconscious. Perhaps, as the apple was eaten, consciousness was born."

"I love it. Now you're all Zen. Give me more, Master Bob."

"Let's just say that before the apple they had no need to think, feel, emote or maybe even eat; everything was done for them. Just like we eat now and give no conscious thought as to how the food becomes blood, cells or bones. It all works without our conscious direction. After the apple, they had decisions to make, and there were consequences for those decisions. That first night must have been frightening." Ann interrupted. "Did they even realize? They ate the apple from the tree of the knowledge of good and evil. It had to be the beginning of knowledge, thoughts and feelings. Knowledge has to relate to separation from God, yet our intellect loves knowledge."

"Knowledge is juicy, like an apple. Think about it, if I eat something now, the cookie, and start directing it to parts of my body to become those parts, I could screw things up royally. I could consciously direct this coffee to my toe and say, 'become a toe nail.'"

They laughed hysterically.

"Maybe in the garden they bit of more than they could chew?"

Bob couldn't resist. "That's trite, Ann."

"Yeah, Bob, but maybe they had a fear of screwing up, just like you in telling your body how to sustain itself. Maybe, just maybe, they were afraid of losing their garden. That old serpent was speaking to them of fear and loss, telling them, 'Taste and accumulate. Protect yourself.'"

"That dirty old snake!"

"The snake is laughing, but without that first bite of apple none of us would even know what evil is. Remember, Bob, it was the tree of the knowledge of good and evil. The question becomes, 'Are you better of knowing or not knowing about evil?'"

"Don't forget, Ann, my friend, the knowledge was good and evil. So, there is a lot of good, too, and probably lots of fun in the separation; lots of juicy apples."

"Would that we could have been happy or accepting in the garden, in God, in 'isness,' but we went in search of knowledge of something other than God, wanting to know intellectually, rather than just being. Maybe it's that the tree will always exist, with evil as a choice, embedded in free will."

"What do you mean, 'isness?'"

Ann took a second. "For me, it's being the

expansion and inclusion of all that is, of God; that the Creator is in the creation. The tempting apple, for me, is fitting the isness or God into my agenda, rather than just being with God and allowing the flow of God. Notice that we have shifted from Adam and Eve to you, me and we. The apple is eternal. Keep choosing God. Give the devil of separation and fear no attention, and don't be seduced by the drama of the unknown. Stay in the isness."

Bob looked serious. "I don't like your phraseology of, 'Don't be seduced by the drama of the unknown.'"

Ann interjected, "The subconscious, the unknown, is leading us, or returning us, to God, to the 'isness.' Don't you always say, 'Trust in God?' Even our dollar bills say it."

At the sound of Bob's pager, the subject was changed.

"Hope it's not a fire" was the extent of Ann's words.

Bob was on his cell phone and was walking down the steps to his car. "They're calling in the troops, Ann. Smoke spotted up by Milk Ranch Point. Gotta go. We'll continue. I like the subject."

He was gone in a flash, and Ann could hear the sound of his old Jeep bumping up the gravel road.

Bob was a great guy, always thoughtful, intelligent, funny, and he had quite a physique for a sixty-something man. His hair was gray and his brown eyes seemed to sparkle and dance simultaneously. He was "Mr. December" for the calendar fundraiser for injured fire fighters and their families. The Rim had been hit hard by fires in past years. Some were acts of nature and some human-caused. Bob, for the most part, was retired, but was always willing to volunteer and, occasionally, was a paid "part-timer."

Ann had a meeting in town. A group of local artists got together to learn about marketing, and to support one another. The local art gallery had managed to stay alive during the recession, but it had been difficult. It was a loving, supportive art community.

3 ART GROUP

*T*he art group was assembled but had not yet started when Ann arrived. One empty seat in the circle was intended for her. See picked up a cushion from another chair and plopped it on her designated aluminum chair.

"Hi, everyone. Sorry I'm a little late. Bob and I were having a great discussion. Actually, we would still be having it, except his pager went off. Smoke on the Rim." Ann had settled in.

The meeting took place in the library annex. The group had access to tables, chairs and a kitchen. Sometimes, people brought their artwork for critique, but, for the most part, they discussed works-in-progress and marketing of finished pieces. A dozen artists sat in a circle, and each shook his or her head in dismay at Ann's comment about smoke on the Rim.

"Thank God for firefighters," Karen said.

"There have been too many fires. Those poor firemen are getting a workout. How's Bob doing?"

Before Ann could answer, Jim stood up and spoke.

"Thinning the forest seems to be keeping the fires at a minimum. It's a good thing they started thinning and stopped worrying about some insignificant animal that might become extinct."

The group was an interesting artist mix, including both environmentalists and hunters. Jim was a hunter who enjoyed photography.

Ann responded to the earlier question about Bob. "You know Bob, ready to go at any moment, and he loves volunteering."

Josephine, nicknamed Jo, entered the conversation. "We have great firefighters."

Alice, president of the group, clapped her hands in a failed attempt to start the meeting.

Jim raised his voice. "We need to get rid of all the environmentalists and let the firemen do their job."

Alice prevailed, slapping her hand against the table. So began the meeting of artists.

Ann's consciousness floated away. She was physically present, but drifting as she thought of Eve as a present-day environmentalist.

4 BOB REMEBERS MEETING LEV

The fire station was a mile down the road from Ann's cabin. Bob could hear the siren of the first-responder truck. Within minutes, he was in uniform and stepping into a back- up truck carrying extra supplies, if needed. He was part of the volunteer corps.

Bob knew the dangers of fighting fires. His previous job was as a paramedic with the Phoenix Fire Department. He had been in Pine for several years and knew the terrain well. Without tripping, he could cross it at midnight under a full moon. When the same terrain was ablaze, all bets were off. It wasn't the same place. He had seen fire travel from tree top to tree top. The animals, if they were lucky, had outrun the flames. Most began running at the first scent of smoke.

As he rode in the truck, Bob thought of his conversation with Ann concerning Eve. He mused that Adam and Eve surely experienced out-of-control fires after they left the garden.

Bob loved working with people. One of his most memorable experiences as a volunteer was responding to an automobile accident involving three cars that were engulfed in flames. Miraculously, everyone survived, but the driver who caused the accident was found to be a drunk driver, Lev. Lev had a reputation as a binge drinker, and a mean drunk. Lev had been arrested at the scene and jailed for resisting officers. He was fired the following day from his driving job at the water department. Something about Lev tugged at Bob.

When sober, Lev was decent and hard-working. Bob couldn't understand why Lev wasted his life on liquor. The event was memorable to Bob because Lev changed for the better after the accident, almost as though the accident had helped him become a better person. Lev had been scared to death at the accident. He made the decision to become accountable, and he joined AA. Both Bob and Jim, from the art group, helped Lev stay afloat by finding part-time jobs for him.

The accident was ten months before, and Lev managed to survive by doing odd jobs, going to AA and trying to put his life back in order. He was eligible for rehire with the water company after a year of sobriety and a clean record. Unannounced sobriety tests would be among the conditions for rehire. It would be a non-driving job and would not pay as well, but it would be a steady job with a good company. Lev was smashing the apple of addiction.

Bob was always prepared for anything. Most fires he responded to, as part of the volunteer crew, were a result of campers not having properly extinguished campfires. On the day in question, he had been called away again to do just that. Campers had left the area without properly extinguishing a fire. It was getting to be an old story. Bob was pleased to be able to do whatever he could to prevent fires.

5 ANN'S JOURNALS CONCERNING EVE

*D*uring the previous year, Ann took a print-making class for the first time. She completed a print that she titled "Mystic Rib." "It represents feminine energy for me," she had told Bob. The print was of a woman with long dark hair, who held an alabaster jar against her chest, reminiscent of Mary Magdalene. A pomegranate in her womb was symbolic of the fertility of Mother Eve. Ann found it interesting that the word pomegranate in Latin is pomum granatum, meaning "seedy apple." Her thoughts returned to Eve. "Mother Eve," what a lovely thought. Ann allowed her thoughts to percolate as she settled herself against the couch cushions.

Ann had a minimal understanding of Carl Jung and archetypes, symbols of universal traits. She knew that dreams contain helpful information. She had heard of parallel universes, and she sometimes put the two together. That night, she wanted to connect in her journaling with a specific archetype, Eve. How cool, she said to herself. Unchartered territory for me. Eve would know about the unfamiliar. After all, she was thrust into a new world.

Ann had considerable experience in journaling her innermost thoughts. She had heard about the still, small voice within. And she had also heard about people with serious diagnoses of hearing and listening to voices in the head. Perhaps it was a forbidden fruit, conversing with her thoughts about Eve, and perhaps she was taking a bite. It was rather late in the evening when she grasped a pen and selected her finest available journal. She lit a candle, settled herself on the couch and uttered a prayer for wisdom and guidance. Then she began journaling, which concerned her perception of Eve.

"Eve, what a beautiful name. What was it like to be with Adam, and the two of you knowing something went incredibly wrong. It doesn't matter who ate the apple first. How did you learn to forgive? Was it the first time you felt anger? Did anger exist before the proverbial apple was eaten? I have so many questions." Ann continued to write, and she allowed the words to flow, as she always did when journaling. On that occasion, however, the words were her perception of Eve.

God's love is so powerful and overwhelming, nothing else matters. The human becomes caught up in the effects. Curiosity in the garden led to exploration with consequences, some positive and some negative. It wasn't a bad journey leaving the garden. There was much to be known on the human journey, not a necessity, but rather a choice. Blame is a human concept. Not forgiving is a cross to bear; that is, if you believe there is something to be forgiven. Being with God is all there is. The details are unimportant. Any human can make details their purpose, if they so choose.

Humans have crosses of one kind or another, until we allow resurrection. "Allow resurrection!" That's an interesting choice of words. We don't cause the resurrection; we allow it into our being. Someone else led the way, namely Jesus Christ. It took the crucifixion to resurrect the light of heaven for human kind.

It was a breath in another world, which began for Adam and for me after that juicy bite. Our gift of intelligence trumped love. Always choose love. Some would say that if we had intelligence we would not have eaten the apple. Through the gift of free will, our intelligence inspired us to pick something different, or something other than God.

Ann was breathless regarding that which flowed through her. She could hardly believe what the pen, when applied to paper, revealed.

It felt as though she had completed a painting, and she stood back in awe at the beauty of her journaling.

6 PRE-CALIFORNIA

Bob invited Ann to dinner shortly before her trip to California. She was happy to spend time with him, but mostly she wanted to share her journaling experience. She dressed in her white jeans and a butterfly tank top. Her body was chubby, and her tall frame hid a multitude of cellulite.

Bob's loud Jeep announced his arrival as he pulled into her driveway. Chopper, already on the deck, barked and ran non-stop off the deck toward Bob.

"Hi, Chopper." The dog crouched on the ground and, with widened eyes, begged for treats. Chopper, a Bichon, whose breed is known for the art of begging, has earned many treats as a result of his skill. Chopper and Bob approached the screen door leading from the deck to the living room. Bob shouted, "Ann, Chopper and I are on the deck." With a panoramic view of Strawberry Mountain, the deck also overlooked a multitude of pine trees.

Ann approached the door. "How about a little white wine with cheese and crackers before dinner? A Sauvignon Blanc or a Pinot Grigio?"

"Sounds good. You choose the wine. Great view out here. Do you ever bring your icon boards out here and paint? No, wait. How do you say it? You write icons, not paint. That's it."

Ann could easily hear him, as the kitchen was a straight shot from the screen door. She opened the wine and prepared the cheese and crackers, with mustard on the side. She knew what Bob liked. "So, you have learned something from me. You're correct, it is writing an icon."

Bob held the door as Ann carried the tray, laden with goodies, onto the deck. "Yeah, mustard." He poured the wine as Ann spoke.

"Too much dust out here to paint. I have prepped boards out here, though." Pointing through the large glass window, she said, "See the icon of 'Jesus not Made from Human Hands?' It's the smallest icon on the mantle."

Bob swirled his wine as he sipped. "Is that the one you wrote up here last summer? This is good wine, my dear."

"Thank you, dear." Ann smiled sarcastically. "That's the board I was sanding when Chopper went crazy and jumped off the deck. There was Chopper at the feet of two large elk with huge racks. They were at that apple tree." Ann pointed toward the apple tree in a neighbor's yard.

Bob finished the food Ann had set before him. "Chopper, you are a wild dog."

"My hands were sticky with rabbit skin glue and full of French chalk, which was blowing all over the place. I kept calling Chopper, and finally I could reach him, pick him up and put him in the house. I got my camera and took pictures of the elk." Ann chewed on a cracker as she spoke.

"The whole thing was rather mystical. Here I am preparing boards as they did in the fourteenth century, with layers of rabbit skin glue and French chalk. I cheated a bit, though, using a hand sander. Remember my Oregon workshop at Mt. Angels, where they taught sacred geometry?" Ann took a sip of wine.

"Wasn't that last July?" Bob asked, "And that's why you were so late getting up here?"

"Good memory. They taught sacred geometry and egg tempura, as the iconographers did in the fourteenth century. And here I am, in the twenty-first century, in the mountains with Chopper and the elk. With my incense burning and chants playing, I was literally transported back in time."

"Sounds eerie, Ann, but something you would love. Pine is kinda like that. Maybe all small towns are that way, but with the trees and Strawberry Mountain, it doesn't get any better. You're lucky the elk didn't kick Chopper like a football."

"I put Chopper in the cabin before anything like that could happen. I don't know if an elk would kick him, but certainly if Chopper had gotten any closer I would have found out. Chopper looked out the window as the two elk stripped the apple tree."

Bob finished his wine. "Those are moments you don't forget."

"Ann nodded her head." One second can make a huge difference. Just one little decision, one little second, can impact creation."

"Uh, oh, I know that tone of voice. You're going somewhere

with this. Shall we head for Italian food? Italian food is good for philosophical discussion, and I know it's coming."

"You know me well. Let's go." She put the dishes and leftovers on the tray and headed toward the kitchen. "You buying tonight?"

"Yeah, and open your own car door, woman." The two patted Chopper simultaneously, and Ann locked the door.

7 MAMA JO'S RESTAURANT

*I*f you've ever been to a good Italian restaurant in a small town, you know the food is probably exceptionally good and the service slow. That was Mamma Jo's. It opened at about 4 p.m. on certain days. But always check on the time, if not a weekend. And if you order pizza, plan on waiting. There is only one pizza oven, and it may take a long, long time. But you can be sure that Mama Jo's pizza is worth waiting for.

Bob took in an exaggerated breath as they entered the restaurant."It smells like heaven in here, with all that garlic."

It was after 6 p.m. on a Friday night, and the place was full, with the exception of one small table in a corner. The hostess/waitress motioned for them to be seated in the corner.

"Perfect," Bob said with a smile. He pulled a chair out for Ann.

She turned toward Bob and bowed. "What

a nice gentleman!"

Bob smiled. "Looks like we'll be here for a while. What type of appetizer would you like?"

"We just had cheese and crackers," Ann said. "Maybe I can get my salad early. What was the special? Do you want pizza?"

Before Bob could speak, the waitress approached them.

"How are you kids doing tonight?" She made mental notes of their orders for salads, veggie pizza and two iced teas. "You know, there's going to be a wait. There are two pizzas ahead of you. I'll bring some antipasto, on the house, with your rolls and salad." She disappeared and reappeared in minutes with tea, salads and a colorful antipasto plate.

"Yum," was Bob's response. "Now, where were we before

you demanded that we go to dinner. Something about the 14th century, I believe, or thereabouts."

Ann dipped a sweet pepper. "When did time begin? Let's go there."

""Define time?"

"Interesting question, Bob. Time is an effect. What was the cause?"

"Effect versus cause, Annie Oakley?"

"Now we're on track. What was the first effect? Were Adam and Eve in pure cause before the apple was eaten?"

Bob set his tea glass down. "Back to Adam and Eve. Then they entered effect, after eating the apple. You think?"

Ann nodded. "In the same way, we are effect. I guess the question is, was the first human, Adam, pure cause? Jesus is the only begotten son. Adam was not of an earthly mother or father. Their children, never mind the incest, were the first children born to earthly parents."

Bob put his salad fork down. "Unless other humans inhabited the earth while they were in Eden. Pass the dip, please. Have you ever thought that there is no mention of Adam and Eve having daughters? More incest!"

"Guess so, Bob. Eve was the only female around. No wonder Cain was so upset. I want to ask Eve if she and Adam had sex before eating the apple? Children are mentioned after the fall. Was sex a punishment? Would they have had children in Eden, anyway? They were childless when they left."

"Eve came from his rib, and if they had children before the apple, surely one of those kids would have left Eden with them. Even if they hadn't eaten the apple, one of those kids down the line would have eaten it. We should have apple pie for dessert." Ann almost choked with laughter.

"Seriously," she continued, "can you imagine what it was like for Eve in that first moment, when everything changed. With apple juice dripping down her chin and the realization began sinking in, of her world turning upside down. Maybe that's when time began."

The waitress placed the pizza on a metal

rack in the center of the table and began clearing away their empty plates.

"Pizza's hot." Bob smacked his lips. "I'll have a Bud.

Want anything, Ann."

Ann nodded. "I'll have more tea, please."

The waitress picked up her glass. "Got it, a Bud and more tea."

Ann served the pizza, placing the largest piece on Bob's plate. "What if we could talk to Eve? What would you want to know?"

Bob chuckled at the thought. "Don't tell me you're Eve reincarnated? I've heard it all!"

Ann continued, "The key word is 'if.' What if?"

"Okay, I'll play. What would I want to know? I'll have to think about that. I'll get back to you on it."

Ann felt he was tired of the subject, which she changed.

They made plans to buy season tickets and attend several concerts with friends at Green Valley Park in Payson.

8 NEXT DAY FIRE TOWER

*T*he following day, Bob was assigned to a fire watch post atop Baker Butte Tower near Strawberry. The driveway to the tower was a mile long, and the task in the tower was to be solo. It was necessary to walk around the top of the tower, or catwalk, using binoculars to spot possible smoke. Bob had a 360-degree view of Rim Country. He enjoyed the solitude of the assignment.

Beside the tower was a small cottage, where the one full-time person assigned to the tower resided. When on vacation, like that day, other firefighters were assigned the job. It was covered full-time during fire season. Bob was to replace Rick, a rookie firefighter.

"Hey, Rick, how's it going?"

Rick reached for Bob's hand. "Couldn't be better, brother. All is quiet and accounted for on the Rim. A few hikers made their way up here. Ground crews were trying to identify four parked cars, and the hikers popped up here."

"Can't be too careful." Both men knew that Homeland Security was part of the everyday agenda.

Rick picked up his backpack and headed for the door. "Have a quiet evening."

"You, too." Bob closed and locked the tower door, which was standard operating procedure. He ascended the stairs and placed his dinner in the refrigerator. It felt like it was going to be a long shift. He opened the door to the ledge that surrounded the top of the tower. At that moment, the two- way radio activated and he heard a familiar voice.

"Hey, Bob, Sgt. Joe Smith here, your friendly connection at command center."

"Reporting for duty, Sarge. Anything I need to know?"

"Been calm, with a small lightning-caused brush fire at

Verde Creek. It was put out in short order. Listen, Rick is a rookie, so look around and make sure everything's in place. He's a good guy, and this was his first shift at the tower."

"Got it, Sarge. Is everything good with you and the family?"

"Couldn't be better. Both kids are in college, and Sara and I are celebrating our 25th anniversary this year."

"Brave woman!"

Both men laughed.

"Speaking of brave, how is your buddy

Ann?"

"She's cool, and always into something."

"Her art is beautiful, especially her icons. Sara wants to

commission her for an icon of Mary Magdalene. I am sure

they'll talk."

"Time for my walk-around, Sarge. Ten-four!"

"Over and Out!"

The machine crackled as Bob pushed the mike button to the "Off" position. He picked up the binoculars again and went out the door. Every half hour, he scanned the horizon. He was thinking as he walked, and he looked around at the vast scene of mountains and trees. Streams of water, appearing as ribbons, passed through the valleys. No buildings were visible. Some valleys had meadows, which he knew belonged to ranchers. But their houses were not visible to the naked eye.

Bob recalled his conversation with Sarge. He knew that Ann would love to do a Mary Magdalene icon. She enjoyed talking with him about Eve, and he realized he would have to bone up on Mary Magdalene, as he surely would have a conversation with Ann concerning both Eve and Mary Magdalene. He was intent on his job of scanning. He remembered his conversation at the Italian restaurant with Ann about Eve. He was going to give Adam and Eve some thought. Tonight's a good night for contemplation. What could be a better place for me to think about Eve?

He made a 360-degree scan, then picked up a pad of paper and began writing. For Ann, he said to himself. "Here I am in a pure, unobstructed forest. This may be exactly what Eve and Adam saw as they descended in consciousness. I'm sitting in a locked tower with binoculars and a two-way radio. They, Adam and Eve, had nothing. Unknowingly, they had just lost everything. If they knew the phraseology, their first words were probably, 'Oh, shit!' They probably experienced night for the first time. And the animals! I wonder if the animals were aware of a shift in consciousness. It's said that man has dominion over the animals and that dominion is one of the greatest gifts of God. In this century, it's unconscionable what some humans do to animals, and great what other humans do for the welfare of animal-kind. Look at Sheriff Joe Arpaio. Whatever his reputation, he rescues abused animals and allows the criminal population to rehabilitate and love them. The criminals rehabilitate and, for many, it's the first time they experience giving love."

Bob took a sip of water, put the writing pad down, got up and continued his walk-around. He had told Ann he would think about Eve. Now, he would surprise her by writing about Adam and Eve. It delighted him that he could impact Ann's heart in that way, or he felt he could.

The sound system crackled, drawing Bob's

attention.

"Bob, you there?" It was Sarge.

"Bob reporting."

"Smoke sighted near Forest Lakes. Keeping you posted."

"Thanks, Sarge. Ten-four. Over and out."

"Ten-four. Over and out."

Bob recognized that Forest Lakes was a good four hours away by car, and not an immediate threat. He focused his binoculars in that direction, but he saw nothing. No such thing as a minor fire, was his thought. He knew that fires like the Rodeo-Chediski smoldered and then burst into uncontrollable flames. He thought of the Rodeo-Chediski, a fire started by a stranded motorist who utilized her cigarette lighter in lighting a small fire to draw rescuers to herself. It worked, as far as rescue, but the little fire ended up burning 450,000 acres and multiple homes. Many never forgave her.

Bob recalled that his buddy Steve had met the woman in a bar. She claimed to have told the rescue workers, when they found her, that the fire was not out and they needed to send reinforcement. Who knows? Bob could not comprehend. He completed his scan, reached for his sandwich, turned on the reading lamp, and grasped a pad of paper. Night was falling, and soon all except the moon and stars would be black.

He decided to entertain himself during his meal break. He thought of continuing to journal about Adam and Eve, because it was popular with Ann and her friends. Instead, he chose to begin a play. Surely many theories existed concerning Adam and Eve. It would be interesting. He chose to begin by writing through the eyes of Eve.

>*Scene I*
>
>*Eve: "Ugh" was the only sound I knew, and it was guttural. I looked to this other, who became known to me as "Adam." In the beginning, we had no language. Everything had been in sublime subconscious, and words were not necessary.*
>
>*Adam: Negative thoughts, shame and judgment did not exist in our previous world. We learned to shape our guttural sounds into words.*
>
>*Eve: That first night was indescribable. Sleep did not occur. Fear overtook us. We clung to one another. It was like rolling in dirt. Nothing felt right. Both of us began to cover our bodies, specifically our genitals. We were hiding.*
>
>*Adam: We didn't understand why we were thrown out of paradise.*

Bob was freaking out. He wanted to connect sex to eating the apple, but that didn't make sense. God wouldn't create something so wonderful as sex and then condemn them for being sexual. There had to be more to the story.

There were fire reports to write, among other things related to his assignment in the watchtower. He had to stop this make-believe, for a while. His lunch period would end soon. He wrote several final entries to his play.

> *Eve: On our first morning, we were awakened by an overwhelming light, sunlight, and it was very warm. We sought shade beneath a tree, not an apple tree. Everything was different. We saw animals roaming about, and they approached us. In the past, we would pet the animals. It was normal and ordinary.*
>
> *Adam: We became as much an enigma to the animals as they were to us. But, now, they recognized our fear. They were afraid of us, and, for the first time, we of them.*
>
> *Eve: All the trees in paradise were fruitful, their bounty unending. We never hungered for anything. Now, our stomachs were empty, and grumbling sounds from deep within could be heard. Hunger was a new experience, and a word we had to learn.*
>
> *Adam: In our hunger, we learned to hunt and kill for food. It was frightening for the animals and for us. Some animals already felt our fear and retreated at our approach. Some were*

docile and shocked by our barbaric attacks. The word "primitive" doesn't come close to describing the experience. Then, as though all animals communicated, which they do subconsciously, the animals began to fear us, and hunting became increasingly difficult. We then developed new hunting methods.

Eve: The trees bore fruit, but it was not as plentiful as in paradise. In paradise, we were vegetarians. But, of necessity, we learned to eat meat. Fire was difficult to come by. In our coldness, we made clothes from animal skins. We experienced winter without being prepared. Huddled together in a cave, Adam, in boredom, rubbed sticks together.

Adam: The cave contained the first fire, and it did not spread beyond the walls. We learned moderation and containment. As a fluke, we began cooking. We had thrown the undesirable parts of the animal we were eating into the fire. The aroma of meat cooking over a fire captured our attention, and tasting the cooked meat was a journey into cooking meat, in much the manner in which you grill today. In paradise, we had dominion over, and respect of, the animal kingdom. After our fall, we still had dominion, but we lost the respect of the animals. We utilized perhaps 95 percent of the animal in the kill. Animals, in their respect for the Creator, knew their purpose now was to help keep humans alive. So, in death, their spirits were subconsciously released in honor, knowing they were to become food.

Eve: The trees seemed to recognize those who entered the forest in honor, and those who came in dishonor. In paradise, all was in honor. Nothing other than honor existed. Trees, of course can't run in fear of fire. Fire often consumed them, as we learned in our feeble attempts at containment. The damage of evil, like that of fire, is a road to resurrection. Many years after a fire, we sometimes returned, and we found previously burned parts of the forest were in various stages of healing and rebirth.

Break was up and his playwriting went into a manila folder, which he took home. When time permitted, and if he were not too sleepy when he got home, he might Google Adam and Eve on the computer! It could be interesting. The remaining time of Bob's shift was uneventful.

9 CALIFORNIA

*B*ob planned to be at Ann's home by noon, so that he could take her to lunch before she headed down the hill to the airport, which was a two-hour drive. He knew Ann liked to drive herself. She often said it was easier for her on her return trip home when she had her car. He pulled his Jeep into her driveway, and soon Chopper was there to greet him. Ann's luggage was on the deck.

"Do you want me to put your luggage in the car?" Bob called out as Chopper circled his ankles. "Chopper knows he's coming to stay with me, don't you Chop?"

"Yeah, he's been excited all morning. Let me lock up, and I'll meet you two at The Brewery." Ann liked their Southwest chicken sandwich and they had outdoor seating, allowing her to take Chopper to lunch. It wasn't something she did often, as Chopper might possibly bother people while they ate. The dog was a good beggar. Ann had a stash of dehydrated veggies in a plastic bag to give to Bob for Chopper treats. She picked up her keys, locked the door and said a prayer for angels to guard her house. She descended the steps and got into her car. Each time she went out of town, she experienced separation anxiety. Her cure was to step into deeper appreciation for her life. She knew she was extremely fortunate to be an artist. Her gratitude expanded to giving thanks for her health, her friends (especially Bob), her dog, and for living in America. Of course, she was grateful to be attending an icon workshop in California.

She pulled her vehicle next to Bob's car in the parking lot. It was easy to spot their table, as Chopper began barking, inviting her to join them.

"Sir, you have a loud dog!"

"You want him? I've been trying to give him away."

Chopper nuzzled next to Ann. Jim and Jo from the art group came in and were seated at the table next to Bob and Ann.

"Do you want to put our tables together?" Jim suggested.

Bob was quick. "Yeah."

The two men shoved the tables together.

Jo smiled at Ann. "I thought you were gone to California."

"I'm on my way. I'm headed to the airport

after lunch."

Jo addressed Bob. "Are you taking Chopper?"

"No, I'm leaving him here for the coyotes."

The men ordered Budweiser, cheeseburgers and fries.

Ann editorialized. "How boring. I'll have the chicken Southwestern sandwich, with fruit and iced tea."

Bob laughed. "Ann, you are predictable."

Jo ordered. "I'll have the prime beef sandwich with fries and a diet Coke." After the waitress left Jo continued, "Ann, tell me about the California artists' workshop. Who is doing it, and what medium will you be using. How do you hear about these things? You always seem to hear about interesting things."

Ann knew Jo rather well. Both belonged to the artist group, as did Jim. Bob, the only non-artist, sipped his beer patiently as Ann shared her story.

"We'll stay at a monastery in Santa Barbara, where we'll learn about egg tempura and Russian icons. The main teacher is a Russian iconographer. Her two apprentices, or assistants, are iconographers, too. I think one is her daughter, if I read the material correctly. All I know is they said beginners are welcome, and that makes me feel good. What are you working on, Jo?"

"Pencil drawings of Pine. I've been parking myself in the middle of nowhere, opening my eyes and drawing. Beauty is everywhere. Even the dead trees constitute masterpieces of grays, with twists and turns, not to mention knotty nubs and branches."

"I've had to rescue her several times," Jim said. "She can't work her GPS, but she has me on speed dial."

They all laughed.

Jo continued. "Be nice to me, Jim, honey. How long have we been together now? Is it two years?"

That was news to Ann.

Jim held up his beer glass in a toast. "Honestly, Jo, I don't know, we just have fun. Here's to love. As long as she doesn't hunt with me, we'll make it. Now, are you two a couple, or not? There are lots of rumors about you two."

Bob saved the day which was his usual. "We're still in the getting-to-know-you phase. We're taking our time, and we like it that way."

A broad smile extended across Jo's face. "I knew you were smart, Ann."

The food arrived and the conversation slowed. Midway through the meal, Jo offered an idea. "When Ann gets back from California, would you all like to come to our house for dinner? Maybe we'll be lucky and Jim will bring some fresh kill home for dinner."

"I'm not big on meat," Ann said with tact and poise, "so I'll bring a pasta salad and cheese, along with fresh bread. I love the bakery in the Ponderosa Market."

The bill arrived and was split between Bob

and Jim. The four headed out the door and said their goodbyes. Chopper led the way. Jo and Jim drove away in Jim's Cadillac, which was graced by antlers on the back end.

That's Jim, Ann thought. He would be a hard one to live with.

Bob looked into Ann's eyes and embraced her. "Drive safely, and call us when you arrive at the monastery. Chopper will worry if you don't."

Ann saluted. "You've got it, Captain."

He opened the door for her, and Chopper started to join her in the car.

Bob picked up the dog. "Not so fast, partner, you're coming with me."

Ann patted Chopper and kissed his head. "Be a good boy for Bob."

Bob laughed. "Just like having a kid!" They kissed and parted.

Driving from Pine to Payson took twenty minutes, and Ann saw only two other vehicles. She arrived early at the airport in Phoenix, had her bags checked and waited patiently at the gate for boarding. Then, she decided to call Bob. "Are you two home safe and sound?"

"Yeah, are you already at the airport?"

"I'm checked in, and am waiting for boarding."

"I was going to wait to tell you, but Sarge is short-staffed, and he asked me to fill in for a month or two. He got permission to pay me for a short-term position. Guess I got good recommendations from Phoenix."

"That's cool. Congrats. You're going to be rich. If Chopper interferes with your schedule, let me know."

"Chopper will be fine. I just have some extra hours.

Besides, Jim and Jo live close, if I need help."

"Be careful out there, Bob. Promise?"

"Always. I've been thinking about Eve. Remember, I promised you I would? So, you know, I keep my promises. I'll be safe. You, too, out there. I hear the Santa Ana Winds are blowing."

"Sounds like weather to me, and I love it. Hey, we're boarding. Later! And thanks for taking Chopper."

"You bet. See you when you get home."

10 IN FLIGHT

Ann settled into her window seat. She liked the window seat, so that she could either nap or read. She would take a book and curl up with it. If she was lucky, the middle seat would remain vacant, and she could spread out. It was only an hour and a half flight. An attractive gray-haired man caught her eye as he made his way down the aisle. He stopped and took the aisle seat, greeting her as he became settled.

Ann returned his greeting. "Good evening." She saw that he was carrying a book, and she tried unsuccessfully to see the title. He turned the book over, and she read the title: "The Black Madonna."

Now, she was very interested. "May I?" she reached out and took the book as he extended it to her. He buckled his seat belt. Ann had hoped the middle seat would remain vacant as she envisioned an interesting conversation with this gentleman. She flipped through the pages of his book and studied the author's name, Malgorzata Oleszkiewicz-Peralba.

"Have you been there, to see the Madonna?" she asked, returning the book to him.

He smiled. "Several times, and you?"

"Not yet, but icons touch me."

The voice of the stewardess was heard on the loudspeaker, with the usual remarks about seat belts and safety measures. Ann placed her purse on the middle seat. "Looks like no one will be sitting here."

"What is it about icons that touches you?"

"The simplicity, the ancientness. They're old, and they seem to have a presence that makes it easy, or easier, to pray. Icons become like spiritual friends, or prayer partners."

"What takes you to Santa Barbara, or do you live there?" "Actually, I'm on my way to an icon writing workshop in Santa Barbara." She couldn't stop smiling. "What are the odds of sitting next to someone who appreciates icons. You wouldn't be going there, as well, would you?"

"I wish I were. My talents are not in the artistic realm."

"Nor mine, but I can pray."

"What do you mean, you can pray? By the way, my name is Rich." He extended his hand.

Ann grasped his hand with a firm grip. "My

name is Ann. Prayer is the element when I write an icon. Each brush stroke, as I have learned and experienced through the years, is a prayer: 'Lord have mercy, Lord have mercy.'" Her hand made imaginary brush strokes in the air to demonstrate her point. She paused in mid air. "Tell me about the Black Madonna."

"I haven't finished the book, but I do know she is powerful and beautiful. As with most icons of the Mother of God, she portrays the feminine. She was attacked and stabbed several years ago and was restored, with some remaining scars. But her powers were never impacted by the brutal attack. There have been many healings, before and after. There is much dedication to her. In fact, I was a recipient."

Ann looked at him in amazement, as though he were an actual icon.

He caught her stare. "You look puzzled, Ann. Or, perhaps you're deep in thought."

At that moment, the stewardess stopped beside them with drinks and snacks. "May I get you two something to drink? Perhaps a bloody Mary?" The woman reached out and grasped the overhead compartment.

"It's a bit bumpy," Ann responded. "No to the bloody Mary, but I will have a spicy bloody Mary mix without the vodka, if I may."

The stewardess put ice in a glass and poured the mix from a can. "You mean a Virgin Mary." She passed the plastic glass and can to Ann. "And you, sir, what may I get for you?"

"Tonic water with a lime, if you have it,

please."

"You bet." She placed Rich's glass on the tray in front of him.

He reached for the glass. "Thank you."

The stewardess continued down the aisle.

Rich took a sip. "Now, where were we? You were painting the air, I believe."

"No, you were about to tell of your encounter with the Madonna, and your healing, if I heard you correctly. Please, there is nothing more that I would want than to hear your story."

"An art historian, I am not. Not by a long shot. Which is why I bought this book. I am, or was, a sports writer by trade, retired and traveling the world. My ancestry is Polish, so one of my bucket-list countries was Poland. My wife was born and reared in France. French and Polish, what a combo! We raised three kids and have four grandchildren, not to mention forty years of marriage.

"Life is a blessing, but I diverge. My wife is a devout Catholic, and she wanted to see the Black Madonna at Jasna Gora. Someone in her rosary group spoke of their journey. We put it on our list of things to do in Poland. Our Lady of Czestochowa is the Black Mother of God who has been in Poland for several hundred years. My wife is more knowledgeable than I."

"This is fascinating to me. Keep going, if you don't mind."

"My wife and I have been to Rome, the Vatican, and to the finest cathedrals of Europe. Nothing ever touched me as deeply as my encounter with the Black Madonna. They have, in Poland, traveling icons that move through the country. The processions are sweet and colorful. The people carry the icon and wear their native dress as they move through town. We saw it once from a distance in a small town. Then we went to Jasna Gora, where the icon resides. We waited in line and had official tickets for the day. It goes the way of spirit, not the way of humans. You know how that goes, I imagine."

"We're talking the same language," Ann interjected. "My heart opens wide as I paint the white in the eyes on the face of an icon. When I was young, I was exposed to icons but have no real recollection. My memory is of very dark pictures, and the darkness frightened me. Now, I can't learn enough. I am the constant beginner. Please go on."

"Prior to our trip, I hadn't felt quite right. My wife, Dee, dragged me to the doctor. And, thank God, she did. My diagnosis, along with the prognosis, was not good. Had it rung true, I would not be on this planet talking with you."

Ann wanted to, but didn't, ask about the specifics. No need conjuring up and regenerating specifics when a healing has occurred.

Rich continued. "The diagnosis is unimportant, other than the fact that I was given six to nine months to live, and that was two years ago. In my opinion, talking about diseases and diagnoses is a waste of energy.

Who wants to focus on what's wrong. Tell the truth, but don't dwell on what you don't want. You know this, too, don't you?"

"Talking about what's wrong all the time makes one feel worse, and, in some philosophies, creates more wrong. The question I ask myself is, does it matter? Can this person I am complaining to possibly change anything? Generally not, which makes it a vent session, and generally identified as such. So, you had a diagnosis, with a prognosis predicting that you would be dead by now. What happened? What changed?"

"In my humble opinion, the Black Madonna graced me with a personal resurrection."

"The power of prayer that I spoke of in writing icons is familiar to you, isn't it, Rich?"

"Very."

A potent period of quiet passed between them. Ann broke the silence. "Are you comfortable giving details?"

"Like when, where, how? No, I don't mind. The story always brings people closer to forgiveness, and to God. My eyes were gazing on the icon and I was praying the rosary, as was my wife. Time stood still, and that which I call energy began to fill my being. It was as though each cell of my being was vibrating, was coming to life. There was a certain amount of heat, but the feeling was very pleasant. It was one of those moments that, at the time, don't seem terribly earth shattering. But, in reality, it was the most life-changing moment of my life, aside from the births of my children. My wife said I didn't move for fifteen minutes. She had tapped me on the shoulder to see if I was all right, but I didn't move. I stared. Truthfully, I don't know exactly what happened. I just know it was the grace of God moving through me. A marching band could have come through the place without any reaction from me. Have you ever experienced anything like that?"

Ann placed her hand on his. "I know the energy you speak of. It's as though something moves through the body. Have you read any of Teilhard de Chardin?"

"I'm not familiar with the name."

"I'll bet your wife has heard of him. He was a French Jesuit, I believe. He speaks of energy. Of course, there is quantum physics, which comes from the pure movement of energy. It's where they say science and religion meet. A novel concept, isn't it?"

Rich shook his head. "You're getting beyond me. I only know what I felt, not why."

The voice of the stewardess was heard on the loudspeaker, announcing their arrival, and asking that passengers prepare for landing.

Rich grasped Ann's hand. "After the experience," he continued, "I returned home and went to the doctor, to begin some pretty focused treatment to shrink the tumor. And, voila, it was gone. The doctor took every X-ray picture imaginable, but found nothing. I told him, 'Doc, quit looking, or you may create something, just to find it.'"

Ann laughed. "I'm grateful to you for sharing your story. And what a wonderful ending! How joyous."

"Remember, Ann, to enjoy every day and every moment. Our son had died two years prior to my diagnosis, and I couldn't find it in me to forgive God. Imagine that! My forgiving God! Not forgiving kills a person. I love God now more than life itself, and I am so grateful to know Jesus Christ in my life. That is all that matters, my friend." With those words, the plane bumped down the runway, and the journey was over. That is, the flight-time segment of the journey.

Ann could not wait to get to the monastery, where she would stay for the icon workshop. She was grateful that she had taken her computer, which was a last-minute decision. One of the first things she wanted to do at the airport, while waiting for luggage, was to quickly look up Jasna Gora, Poland.

On Wikipedia, she read the following about Jasna Gora Monastery in Poland: The Jasna Gora in Czestochowa, Poland is the most famous shrine to the Virgin Mary in Poland and is the country's greatest place of pilgrimage; for many, its spiritual capital. The image of "Black Madonna of Czestochowa," to which miraculous powers are attributed, is Jasna Gora's most precious treasure. (1 Czestochowa official website@Urzad Miastra Czestochowy

Slaka 11/13, 42-217 Czestochowa

retrieved 208-10-22.)

Founded in 1382, by Pauline Monks, who came from Hungary at the invitation of Wladyslaw, Duke of Opole, the monastery has been a pilgrimage destination for hundreds of years. It contains the most important icon of the Virgin Mary in this part of Europe. The icon, depicting the Mother of God with the Christ Child, is known as the "Black Madonna of Czestochowa" or "Our Lady of Czestochowa," which is widely venerated and credited with many miracles (2Jasna Gora @1998-2008).

Ann was so excited by that which she read, she had a difficult time focusing on locating her luggage. She made her way to the cab stand, hailed a cab, and made it to the monastery in time for registration and dinner. She reminded herself that often one learns something far more valuable than that which one originally came to study.

11 WORKSHOP BEGINS

*T*here were twenty students and three teachers. One of the teachers was Polish. Ann made a mental note to spend time with her in order to learn her views on the Black Madonna.

The first night was an introductory time. When the time came, each student was able to choose one of the eight icons presented to paint. The choices included angels, saints, a Madonna with Child and the Black Madonna.

Ann couldn't contain her enthusiasm as she selected the Black Madonna. She spoke aloud:"Just last night, on the plane ride here, we talked about the Black Madonna, and now it's here, presented as a choice for me to write."

Ann noticed scars on the face of the Black Madonna, and she recalled having heard from Rich that the icon was brutally attacked with a knife during a battle. She found that, despite its restoration, the scars remain, and it continues to be painted with scars.

The theme of all icon workshops, Ann had learned, was that the icon points to God. The icon, in and of itself, is paint and board and, of itself, has no power. Ann was reminded of a sermon she head at a church in Payson the previous Sunday. The priest addressed the issue of Catholics placing statues of Mary in their backyards. Neighbors had complained to a Catholic homeowner that the statue in their backyard was a false idol because it was a statue. The congregant had brought the complaint to the attention of the priest and it became part of his sermon.

The sermon went on to include that one worships only God and not false idols. The priest brought up the history of the iconoclasm and the fact that all images, both icon and statue, were destroyed in one particular time period. That was wrong, and was later reversed, he said. Most American Catholics venerate statues and, the Orthodox, the icons. Veneration is part of Catholicism. In the same way, we venerate pictures of our deceased parents, of family members and friends; we venerate icons. Ann perceived that from the priest's sermon. Ann was amazed that all the dots regarding icons seemed to be connecting.

She spent time during several meals at the workshop with a student of quantum physics. Their discussions centered around energy, tangential and spatial. Much like a cross, the two energies connect. Much like the physical and the spiritual the two energies cross. Ann felt her experience of the energy deepen with discussion.

12 WATER SITUATION

Word spread through the Pine community that the water in the system was contaminated and should not be consumed. This was a shock, as the community had purchased the water rights, and everything appeared to be running smoothly; better than it had in some years. The problem concerned a mechanical problem that caused dirt to enter the water pipes. Everyone in the area was allotted three free gallons of water, to be picked up at the water office. It was estimated that the system would be repaired and that clean water would flow again within three days.

Some people felt there was a possible sabotage of the pipes, and some thought the water supply was low, which dangerously lowered the water level. If the latter were true, the built-in alarm didn't work. Supposedly, when the water arrived at a low point, an alarm would notify authorities, who could remedy the situation. Water shortages were always a fear in mountain communities. Such communities support one another. People from Show Low had driven a long distance to help with distribution. One of the helpers was Lev's cousin, Stuart.

Stuart was a no-nonsense ranch hand who knew the Rim like the back of his hand. He was a church-going man with a bright future. His wife was a teacher in the local school. Bob, in helping Sarge, had been assigned to help with water distribution. He knew Stuart through 4-H Club connections. The two ended up in the same place.

"Hey, Stuart, is that you? What are you doing in these parts? Are you lost?"

"I'm checking on guys over here in Pine. Word is that you don't know what you're doing."

The two men hugged and slapped one another on the back.

"How can I help, Bob? Actually, I'm here as a volunteer. I'm official."

Bob smiled. "Great, are you staying with Lev, or do you need a place to stay?"

"I'm staying with Lev. I left him a message, and I'm sure it'll be all right. So, what do you want me to do?"

"You can help distribute water. Each person gets three gallons. Just get their names and which community they're with, such as Cool Pines, Portals. See my list, here?"

At that moment a truck loaded with

hundreds of one-gallon water bottles pulled up, and all those available began unloading.

Bob returned to the firehouse, next door, to check in, and he looked at the schedule for the day. It was going to be a busy one, and, as always, water shortages made everyone uncomfortable. Bob remembered the days when the water supply was dependent upon local ponds. The location of the local ponds had stood for years and was now replaced by big houses in a fancy development. There were back-up tanks, suitable for fighting fires, but not for drinking. Hikers knew water was throughout the area. Fossil Springs was lush, but Phoenix had most of the water rights. Three new water wells throughout the area had been developed by the new board. The wells extended down between 1,000 to 1,200 feet, replacing those at only 500 feet. Supposedly, they had tapped into the Fossil Springs water supply.

The forest was closed for recreational use because of drought. Things were relatively under control. The sky was clear and no lightning storms were predicted. Storms without lightning would be good, but none were expected. Bob had seen many Manzanita bushes explode when ignited. He knew that an unattended campfire is an extreme danger in a dry forest.

13 LEV AND STU

*L*ev was 38 and built like a tank truck. He was a high school athlete before dropping out of school in the 11th grade. He was the eldest of eight children. Both of his parents drank to excess. Lev carried a great deal of responsibility for the younger children. He took on a part-time job to help with family bills. He learned to cope with stress by drinking liquor, which progressed to drug usage. Money was in short supply, so drugs were limited. He got into trouble with the law and deservedly spent six months in the county jail as the result of a three-car accident caused by him. Bob had responded to the accident.

All that was behind Lev. He had finished a rehab program, found religion and was doing his best to stay out of trouble. A knock sounded at the back door, and Lev made his way there. "What fool goes there?"

"Cousin Stuart, you no good son-of-a-gun."

The door flung open and the two cousins embraced. "Got your message. You know, you're always welcome.

How's the family? I don't have any beer, but how about a Coke. You know, Cola?"

"No beer? You kiddin' me? Are you sick?"

"It's one day at a time, you know. I'm on the wagon. I didn't bother telling too many people, but I joined AA, Alcoholics Anonymous. Ever heard of them?"

"Lots of souls have found their way through AA," Stuart said. "Cola sounds good. Is it cold?"

Lev opened his refrigerator, popped two cans of Pepsi and handed one to Stuart.

"My life was spiraling downward, and I had to do something. It's a lot of hard work, but AA is a great support group. There are meetings every day. Actually, I'm happier than ever. I just can't be around drinking right now."

"Hey, I get it. Through the years, I worried about you. But you didn't seem like a person who would listen."

"I wasn't, and I still don't. Promise not to laugh?"

"Maybe. No, I won't. I'm so gosh-darn proud of you Lev.

You're the man! I won't laugh." The men clicked cans.

"Okay, Stuart, I am telling you, I pray." There was a long silence. "I pray to a higher power, and something happens. Do you remember that Sunday school teacher, Miss Jo? She was always after us boys to pray, and I was always sneaking out or laughing at her."

"Oh, yeah, isn't she an artist? A sketch artist, I believe."

"Yeah, and a good one. Her boyfriend is a great guy. Did you ever meet Jim? Crap, I don't even know his last name. He's big into hunting. He gives the meat away to the poor. He's given me elk in the past."

"No, I don't know him. Isn't it funny how people stay in our lives? After all these years, you remember a lady for her prayers."

"I look at her boyfriend, Jim. He's a great guy. He helped me with a job last week, and he didn't want no money from me. It almost made me cry. I look at the two of them and I know prayer has to work."

"Maybe he's just glad you stopped drinking and he wants to help you."

"Maybe. You know, it's this stuff about one day at a time. I don't want to talk about it and have people ask stupid questions, like, 'Will you ever drink again?' I feel pressure."

Stuart placed his hand on Lev's shoulder. "I hear you, bro. You hungry? Let's go eat. My treat. Besides, you can't cook."

"That's changed, too," Lev said. "Just kidding. But I'm close to being rehired by the water company. I'm waiting for the dust to settle and my name to be cleared."

"Great! Would it be full- or part-time?"

"Full-time, with benefits. Imagine that! I

may even get a life of my own, with a partner. You know, Stuart, I've always looked up to you. You have a happy life, with a wife and kids."

"If you want it, it will happen. Keep working. I always knew you had it in you. Just remember, living with a woman isn't easy. Remember, she's always right! With that thought in mind, you'll be successful."

The door slammed behind them, and they headed for Stuart's truck.

"Since you're buying, Stu, let's go to the Strawberry Lodge. Tonight is prime rib night."

"Sure, that sounds good." Both got into Stu's truck. "Is it hard for you to be in some of these restaurants? I mean, after you got drunk there, and all?"

"No, cuz I don't remember. I don't go to restaurants much unless wealthy relatives come to town."

Both men laughed.

"Seriously, Stu, being drunk all the time is like living in a parallel universe."

"What, you getting all wacko on me, or metaphysical, or whatever they call it?"

"A person learns a lot in AA. In my drunkenness, I have no awareness of my physical world. I should say 'had,' past tense. That was good for me, cuz my physical state was so miserable."

"I get it. In your drunken state, it was like being in another world."

"Bingo! I'm working on healing myself. The more I heal, the better I like me and my world.

Then, I don't have to travel to drunken land."

"Just don't go visiting Mars or the moon, you hear?" Stu pulled into a parking place. "Time to eat." Both men got out.

Lev wanted to share more, but he knew it was not the appropriate time. He had shared enough for one night. Besides, talking about AA had been a big step. That was enough.

"Just one thing, Stu." Lev placed his arm around his cousin as they entered the restaurant. "It feels really good not to be judged by you. Thank you, cous

14 JIM AND JO'S ANNIVERSARY

*J*im's body had an inbuilt GPS system. His brain could calculate without his conscious direction. He always knew, without a compass, where to step and in what direction. It was as easy as breathing for him. He stood at 6 feet, 4 inches, and weighed 250 pounds; yet, he was as gentle as a kitten. His voice was rough, deep and commanding. Domestic animals responded to his gentleness. Jo's cat often wound himself around Jim's heels and purred on his shoe. It made Jo wonder about him.

"Jim, you are such a big, burly guy. How come you're such a teddy bear with little animals?"

"They know I'm tender-hearted." He gave her a hug.

Jo pressed her 5-foot, 3-inch frame against him. "How does that work?" You're a hunter; you hunt to kill animals. Don't they sense that?"

"That's just it, Jo, my dear, animals know that I hunt for food to eat. Some hunt only for the sake of killing, and they disregard the meat. But I utilize even the skins from my kill. There's no waste."

"What about the skins?"

"I sell the skins to Henry, over in Prescott, and he uses them in drum making. He told me that each skin is blessed because he's a medicine man. He stretches the skin over the drum mold and whispers to the spirits. Henry explained to me that each time anyone beats the drum, the stretched skin is drummed and the spirit of the animal is remembered. Isn't that beautiful? Just like you." He bent down and gently kissed her.

"You big goof! I'll bet your poker buddies would never believe me if I told them that story."

Both laughed. The two of them had been living together for two years. Both were in their sixties and felt no need for a marriage certificate. They were opposites in many things, but they agreed on that.

Jo was packing her sketching bag and looking for her favorite folding chair.

"Today should be a perfect day for me to sketch on the mountain." She hesitated in the kitchen, staring into the refrigerator. "I wish someone would invent a way for me to order lunch and have it delivered to wherever I end up."

"That, little darling, would be a miracle. For

the most part, you don't know where you are."

"I hate it when you're right. But I get busy finding my spot and forget how I got there."

"Make sure you have your cell, and carry your GPS. I know, I know, you don't use it, but I can read your way points from it."

"My hero!"

"I hear the sarcasm."

"I trust in that Almighty Spirit who guides the smallest of birds. Surely He can guide me, if I listen. That's my biggest challenge, listening to Spirit rather than my ego."

Jim could hardly contain himself. "What did you do before me? How did you survive?"

"That's my point, I did just fine. I'm very grateful for you.

You know, that's what Ann is always talking about: be grateful, be grateful."

"Eternally grateful, if I remember right. I like her, but I don't understand her relationship with Bob. Are they together like a couple?"

"Ann says they're getting to know each other, but nothing serious. She's a deep thinker, always talking about spirit stuff. It gets me that she talks about being grateful for negative stuff. 'A treasure in everything,' she'll say. I work on it."

"No wonder Bob keeps his distance."

Jo grimaced. "You're kidding me, and I know it. You pray every day. You trust in something."

Jim shook his head.

Jo continued, "I'm on my way to the East

Verde River, not the mountains. I'll park there, of Highway 87, and walk along the river for a distance."

"What are you looking for?"

"Today, maybe a bird or a tree will catch my fancy. I'll see where Spirit takes me. What are you doing today, my love?"

"I'm going to go help Lev with a side job again today, as soon as I finish with this computer."

"Lev?"

"Yeah. I know he's been a drunk, but hopefully he's turned a new leaf. He takes on a lot, hoping to pay his bills. He needs the money, and I have a little time to help him. You be careful there at the river."

"I will, Jim, and maybe tonight we can head to Sidewinders for dinner and celebrate our second anniversary of living together. I think a blues band is playing."

"Sounds good. Love you."

Jo had lost a son in a terrible automobile accident four years before. She never parted ways from a loved one without saying, "I love you."

Jim didn't object, and he smiled. "Love you more."

15 ANN AT HOME

After an uneventful flight home, Ann landed at Sky Harbor Airport, Phoenix, exactly on time. She replayed her conversation with Rich concerning the Black Madonna. The serendipity of talking about and then writing the Black Madonna freaked her out. Her mind was filled with thoughts.

Her icon was safely packed in her luggage.

The airport was crowded, and she found a quiet corner. She dialed Bob's number, with no response. Her cell phone rang within seconds. It was Bob.

"Hi, Ann. You called. Are you at home?"

"Not yet, but I'm getting my car and heading up the Beeline. How's Chopper?"

"Ornery, as ever. He's good. You gonna ask about me? How I am?"

"Okay, how are you, Bob?"

"I'm feeling great. Don't know if you heard,

but we had a water problem. Some thought it was a shortage, some that the pipes were sabotaged. And some don't know/don't care, cuz it's all fixed, and we're good to go."

"Doesn't sound like it caused much of a problem."

"If you count not having water for three days not a problem, then you're right."

"Did they transport water in?"

"They couldn't because the pipes were letting in dirt. They say it was a mechanical thing. We can talk when you get up the hill."

"I better get started up the hill. I'm a little tired, and it's a two-hour drive."

"Tell you what; you gave me a key to your house, in case Chopper needed anything. Why don't I put some of my famous left-over veggie lasagna in your frig when I drop off Chopper?"

"You're one of a kind!"

"I've gotta leave for work in about an hour. I'll tell

Chopper you're on your way."

"Sounds good. Thanks again, Bob. I want to take you to dinner after I recuperate."

"I'm glad you said that. Jim and Jo invited us for dinner

next Saturday. There are some other people, but wanted to check with you before I accepted."

That'll be fun. Find out what I can bring and who else is going?"

"I know Alice from your art group is going, and some others. Lev was invited, but he may not make it. I think some people are suspicious about him and think he sabotaged the water system. Most think it's bullshit, but accusations take a toll. He's with AA now, you know, after that bad accident."

"AA, is that 'after the apple,' or Alcoholics Anonymous?"

"Very funny! Hurry up and get home. We can talk tomorrow. Cool?"

"Cool. My water is good?"

"Your water is fine. No worries. Drive carefully, and no speeding."

"Got it. Bye, Bob."

"Bye."

Chopper heard her car pull into the cabin driveway. He was beside the door and was not barking. Ann opened the door, and he rushed to the side yard. He was on the scent of a deer or a cat. She had only one word to say, "treat," and he was back inside.

"You love food more than anyone I know."

Chopper begged for more.

Ann went into her bedroom and unpacked. Most of it was dirty clothes, all bundled together in a laundry bag. Inside the few clean clothes was her icon of the Black Madonna. Carefully, she unwrapped it, held it in her hands and said a prayer. She found a stand and placed the Madonna on the dining room table.

She remembered that Bob had said he would leave food for her in the refrigerator. True to his word, she found left- over lasagna, a salad, and a piece of apple pie from the bakery. She laughed as she removed the Saran from the pie. I'll begin with this.

Ann awoke early the following morning, before 4 a.m. Not wanting to disturb Bob so early, she made the five-minute drive to the post office and picked up her mail. She thought of the fact that there is no home delivery of mail in Pine, no stoplights and just a few stop signs. Her mailbox was full, with mostly junk mail. There was a notice of a larger delivery, with a key to another box. She opened the other box and found a book from Amazon. She tore open the package and found it contained "The Black Madonna," which she had ordered. It was the book Rich had on the plane. She knew how she would spend that day.

After leaving the post office, Ann went to the Early Bird Cafe for breakfast. From a distance, she saw Lev leaving the cafe. She remembered what Bob had said about Lev's possible involvement in the water situation. It seemed unfathomable that Lev would have anything to do with sabotaging water, no matter how drunk he might have been. She made a point of waving to him. Inside the restaurant, she felt at peace. Her new book was in her hand, ready to be read during her meal. She had just ordered eggs, when her cell phone rang. It was Bob.

"Good morning Ann."

"Same to you. You're up early." She sipped her coffee. "Where are you? I stopped by your house, and you were already gone."

"I didn't want to awaken you. I thought maybe you had
worked late."

"Understatement. Where are you?"

"Early Bird, having breakfast. Why, what's going on? I hear something in your voice."

"I'm on my way. Order coffee for me. I'm waiting for a call, so it'll be quick."

"Okay."

Bob had already clicked off.

Ann's breakfast was set before her. She put her book down and caught the eye of the waitress. "Oh, thank you. And another cup of coffee for my friend, who's on his way."

"You got it."

"Thanks." Ann cut into her hash browns with a fork and the steam rose. The warmth felt good in her mouth.

The door to the Early Bird opened, and Bob walked in.

"Morning." He waved to some of the regulars he knew as he
made his way to Ann's table.

The waitress delivered his cup of coffee.

Bob held up his right hand in acknowledgment. "Thanks."

"Okay," Ann began, "what gives?"

"Jo is missing."

"What?" Ann choked as she swallowed a bite of egg.

"What do you mean, missing?"

"She went out sketching late yesterday

afternoon and left a note for Jim, in case he came home early from Heber. Basically, it said not to worry, that she'd be home by dark. He had no idea she was missing because he got home late, very late. He was in Heber at a party for his hunting buddies and stayed longer than he had intended. Actually, he was going to stay the night in Heber, but when Jo didn't respond to his messages or answer her phone, he headed home. He knew something was wrong. It was well after midnight when he got home, and no Jo."

"Where did she go? I don't understand. Did they talk?" "Here's what I know. She left the house at around 3 p.m. yesterday and left a note on the table. The note didn't say where she was going, only that she was going and would be home by dark. You know cell phones up here, there are lots of places without reception. He didn't get home until the wee hours this morning. He's kicking himself for not coming home earlier. I'm waiting for Jim's call. The sheriff is looking for her car now.

"We've got crews from Search and Rescue on standby. She could have gone a couple of directions. We've gotta find the car. Jim is getting his stuff together. He doesn't know it yet, but he and I are driving together. I wanted to tell you in person."

The waitress refilled his coffee cup and that of Ann.

"How is Jim doing? Did you know this last night when we talked on the phone?"

"Jim, he's mad at himself for not being home earlier. Even if he was, she would still have been missing, only the sheriff would have been called sooner. She has her cell phone, but no response. He's organized his hunting buddies, and they're all waiting for a call, with directions on where to meet. Did I know when we talked? No, but shortly after he got home Jim started calling around. He called me, looking for you. He was calling everyone to see if someone else was with her. He couldn't reach her by cell. Technically, she isn't considered missing until 24 hours have passed. You know how it goes. They say she may have wanted to be alone, maybe ran away."

"How can I help?"

"He has his RV ready to go as soon as the sheriff gives the location. Health-wise, Jo is strong. It's just, who knows whether she's hurt, or what wild animals are around. She could have fallen and broken a leg, with no way to contact anyone."

"I wonder if she has a whistle."

"Jim says she does. Jim has specifically asked you to pray, and anyone else who may have prayer chains has been asked to pray. Alice has called all the members of your art group."

Both sat in silence.

Ann looked at her book, "The Black Madonna," and knew it would be on a back burner.

Bob's cell phone rang. "Yeah, Jim, Clover Creek." He cupped the phone and whispered to Ann, "They found her car at Clover Creek." Bob uncupped the phone. "I'm on my way. Wait for me."

He got up to leave. "I'll keep you posted, Ann."

"Should I go out there? Can I help, or would I be in the way?"

Bob knew Ann was a good hiker, but certainly not the caliber of the Search and Rescue squad. "I don't know what to tell you. Come out and support Jim. I don't think she's that far in. It probably got dark, was raining hard, she found shelter, and she stopped. If she didn't stop, and if she continued, she may have fallen. They'll find her this morning."

"Why would she go out so late in the day yesterday? That's not her normal."

"I'm on my way now. Later." He kissed her on top of the head.

15 JO GOES SKETCHING

*J*o wakened late in the morning. They had stayed out late the previous night, dining and dancing at Sidewinders. Both celebrated a bit too much. She was tired. She knew Jim was gone on his way to Heber. As was his custom when he awoke early for hunting, he left her a sweet note next to the coffee pot. She went into the kitchen, feeling comfortable in her bathrobe. Nothing was on her agenda for the day. She thought of Jim and his circle of friends. There were always five or six men who wanted to hunt. Jim seldom hunted alone. Jo longed for a circle of sketching friends who would get up early and search for the best sketch location.

Jo opened her dining room door that led to the deck.

The phone rang, and she thought it was probably Jim.

He greeted her. "Hi, honey."

"Good morning. I'm just opening your note."

"You slept in?"

"Yes, I did, and it felt good."

"You didn't miss me waking you up?"

"Of course, I did, and you'll wake me tomorrow. Did your buddies all show up in Heber?"

"We're all here and accounted for, except Billy. He's going to be so surprised. He thinks we guys are just getting together for lunch. The photo album is beautiful. I'm glad I made 25 copies of it, so his kids and grandkids will have copies."

"Your photography is always amazing."

"You're sweet, Jo, and prejudiced. Keep it coming."

"It's not every day your hunting buddy of 50 years retires with a photo book of his hunting history. Only you would have all those years of pictures and would have saved them."

"You know, he was the one to encourage me in photography. He always said I had more energy for the camera than for the kill."

"Was there much traffic?"

"Only through Payson. I picked up all the albums when the store opened, then headed to Heber."

"I'm glad everything was ready on time. Is everything set at The Red Onion for the party?"

"Just waiting for Billy. One of his buddies brought some old videos that we'll be showing.

I don't know what time I'll get home tonight. Probably late. You know how these 'guys-only' celebrations go."

"You all think the little women want you home by dinner.

Truth be known, we women will be planning our own fun day.

Maybe we'll spend the day, unencumbered, at the casino."

Both laughed.

"Jo, you are too much! How did I get so lucky?"

"Yeah, you are lucky."

"So, what would you plan for a day without me? Or, how did you say it, unencumbered by me?"

"That's just it, my love, my days are all planned like that anyway."

"I'm getting the signal that Billy's arriving. Good thing we had everyone here an hour early. Gotta go, honey. Love you. Have fun, whatever you do today."

"Love you."

"See you tonight Jo."

"Drive safely, Jim. Remember, we talked, and you promised to spend the night up there if you drank."

Jo went onto the deck and enjoyed relaxing in her bathrobe. At 1 o'clock, she progressed to the newspaper and read the time for the full moon rising. She began thinking about shadows and moonlight. On full-moon nights, she kept the blinds in the bedroom open and watched the moon as it rose and fell mysteriously into the forest that backed their home in Pine. It seemed to her that the full moon in their mountain community functioned much like a streetlight.

Being out in pitch black would not be her thing, but "Wouldn't it be lovely to sketch in the moonlight?" she said aloud. The wheels in her mind began turning. She thought of all the lovely animal photography Jim had done, and of the fact that he was never afraid to try something new. This would be her something new. She looked at the clock and gave herself an hour, or until 3 o'clock to get ready and be out the door. She could explore and find a location. When darkness approached, or no later than 8 p.m., she would head toward home. She would get a little moonlight even if only driving home. "Heck, I'll have five hours. That's more than I sometimes give myself in daylight." A plan was hatched, and she was in the shower.

She considered calling Jim, but she knew he would be in the middle of the party. So, she decided to leave a note. In all probability, she would return home before he arrived.

When those men start trading hunting stories, they lose track of time. She left a note for him. She didn't indicate where she was going, as she didn't know. This would be her "something new"; to just head out, unencumbered. She reached Highway 87 and turned north, toward Strawberry. She continued past Strawberry. The elevation approached 7,000 feet, and it was much cooler than in Pine. The coolness was a bonus. Ahead, on the left, she saw what looked like a parking lot and a wooden billboard. She thought that perhaps the billboard might provide a map of the area. So, with her turn signal blinking, she turned left onto a forest road. It was a weekday, and traffic was light.

She got out of the car and approached the billboard, only to find it did not provide a map. It gave information on water development for the area—a riparian area—and it gave all the documentation and progress to date. She decided to remain parked there and to follow the road by foot up the hill. She observed several RVs in the area, which she passed as she walked. And she was aware of many turn-of trails.

With sketching equipment in hand, she said a prayer and headed down a trail to her right. She had a gallon of water, which added weight, but she felt strong. She waved to a couple who appeared to be packing up to leave the site. They returned her gesture. She found that RV people were always friendly. Jim liked RVing, but she did not. She often told him, "I like a full bathroom." He heard her and didn't push it. She was still a city girl.

She felt that her hiking boots and stuffed backpack made her look like a legitimate hiker. She was glad she had decided to take her small sketch pad. After a half hour, she found herself in a round parking lot with four cars. There was a fenced area with a metal walk-through gate. The sign read, "West Clear Creek Trailhead." It was public land, and she entered.

She followed the trail as it circled to the right. Her heart skipped a beat as she viewed the beauty. Meadows of clover unfolded next to rocky cliffs, with lush green trees everywhere. It was evident there had been a lot of rain. The trail seemed to continuously unwind. Nestled within the little piece of heaven flowed a gentle creek that stretched along the path. She saw an old cement bridge, and she remembered stories of the old Highway 87 and the fact that the new road had bypassed old rugged portions. This must be Clover Creek, she thought, but the sign read "West Clear Creek."

She found a perfect view of the bridge and began unpacking her bag and setting up. She picked up her cell phone and dialed, to leave a message for Jim on their home phone.

What? No service. Crap, was her thought. She tucked the cell phone back into her pack and began sketching the bridge. Four people emerged from the denseness of the forest. They saw her long before she saw them. She lost track of everything when she placed a pencil in her hand and began to sketch.

"Hello," the first of the two women called.

"Oh, hello. I didn't see you coming."

"We didn't want to startle you. How are you?"

"How could I be anything other than wonderful, surrounded by all this beauty."

The other woman and two men following the women caught up and exchanged greetings with Jo. One of the men, who introduced himself as John, remained behind the other three as they moved on.

"You must be an artist. May I look at your sketch?"

She extended her sketch pad toward him. "I've barely started."

"I paint, and I wish I had brought my paints and pad with me."

"Do you want some paper and pencils?"

"No, thanks, though. We have a dinner party tonight, and then we'll head back to Phoenix early tomorrow. If I were staying, I'd be back. Have you hiked this before?"

"No, but I've heard it's fairly easy. Was it?"

"Oh, very easy, but a mile into it, on the left, is a circle of stone slabs around an old-looking fire pit. The slabs are set up like low chairs, with a stone seat and an almost-matching slab for a back. There are like seven or eight chairs. It looks so mystical and old, if you believe in that sort of thing."

The other three members of his party were patiently waiting for him.

"I've got to go. What you've got looks good." He handed the pad back to her.

"Thanks. How far down did you say the stone circle is?"

"Not quite a mile."

"Thanks. Bye."

"Enjoy," he said as he departed.

Two other hikers were exiting the trail, and they exchanged waves with Jo. Another single hiker entered and waved from a distance. He moved rapidly, though packing a large, heavy-looking backpack with what appeared to be a tent.

Jo kept thinking about the old stone circle John had mentioned. She looked at her watch. It was 4:30. She had barely started her sketch of the bridge, but she rationalized she could come back another time to do it.

I'm going for it. She packed up and proceeded down the trail.

16 NOT QUITE A MILE

*T*he trail, which crisscrossed a creek, was fairly easy. The scenery became increasingly more intriguing. In some places, the overgrowth hid the path. Somehow, the trail always emerged, even when there were large rocks and fallen tree stumps. On one occasion, she found it necessary to go down on her hands and knees and climb under a fallen tree. Again, she calculated in her head the needed time to exit, in order to arrive home before dark.

At 7 p.m., no matter what, I'm, heading out.

She was fully aware that in leaving at 7 p.m. she would get back to the car by dark, but certainly not home before dark. She depended on the working of her cell phone when she reached the car. Then, she could call Jim. She felt relief that her car was parked by the main road and would not be difficult for her to find. She tried to set her phone alarm to ring at 7 p.m., but it didn't work. Her watch didn't have an alarm, but she would keep looking at it for a time check.

She removed a bottle of water from her pack and perched herself high on a rock. In all directions she saw nature at its purest. From a distance away, she heard cows. She had known they frequented the area, as evidenced by the dried cow manure she had seen. Occasionally, a gentle breeze embraced her

This must be what heaven is like. Come on, old lady, let's get going. She was back on the path, and figured she had gone a mile. But she saw no stone circle. The trail led down to, and crossed, the creek. She looked up the embankment and saw the tops of what appeared to be two stone slabs extended above the brush. She veered to the left, and before her was the stone circle.

The fire pit in the middle was lined with stones and appeared to have been used recently or perhaps within the past year. Eight flat stones encircled the fire pit. Five of the eight had flat stones propped up, similar to the backs of chairs. Clearly they were intended for sitting.

How old is this circle? she wondered. The ancient rocks were much like others she had seen on the trail. She was in a canyon of rocks and trees, extending as high as one hundred feet above her, with a comparatively small stream gurgling beside her.

"What a picture!" she said aloud. She

unloaded her pack, for a second time in the past couple of hours, and she determined her optimum location for a sketch. Before beginning, however, she felt the need to sit on one of the stone chairs. They were low to the ground, and she felt a sense of empowerment. Are these old, or did campers or hikers lay them out like this? She closed her eyes and felt a calm energy, the reason she loved nature.

She got up, moving more slowly than when she got down. Gravity and old age, she thought.

Pencil in hand, she finally began sketching. The shades of gray were all there, and long shadows were reaching out to touch her toes. A rustle in the brush drew her attention. Jo had a tremendous dislike of snakes, and her first thought was of such a creature. Upon closer scrutiny, the rustling sound had come from something with feathers, like a large bird.

What is it? With curiosity, she followed. Obviously, she wasn't going to finish a sketch that day. Curiosity had her.

Huge boulders surrounded the creek.

She found the trail to be the most beautiful she had been on in a long time, and exploring it caused her creative juices to flow. At the next bend in the trail, she found the boulders to become increasingly larger. Her boots were serving her well, but she found she had left her hiking stick at the stone circle.

The bird was nowhere in sight. She felt she had missed her opportunity. Maybe the bird was an injured eagle. She didn't know whether eagles were in the area. Jim would have known.

She looked at her watch. Oh, my, it's 7 o'clock!

She believed she was at least 20 minutes from the stone circle. The distance wasn't that far, but the tediousness of climbing boulders would slow her. Thank God I didn't go farther.

She felt a level of anxiety rise within her. She knew she was at least an hour away from being able to call Jim. Just a little more, she thought, as she continued cautiously, weaving in and out among the boulders. It was still daylight, but clouds were gathering over the Rim, and sunlight was dimming. A gentle rain began to fall.

My sketch pad will get wet. With increased anxiety, she became more motivated. As she descended from the last boulder, her foot became stuck in a crevice, and she fell, head first, losing consciousness.

17 SOMETHING IN THE NIGHT

*I*n the past, Jo had wondered if people in a coma felt pain. They appeared to be in a deep subconscious state. Her first glimpse of consciousness after her fall was a searing pain moving up her right leg. Then the pain of her head and twisted body began to register. Her body, she felt, was upside down. A full moon was hidden behind clouds, and the night was pitch black.

"Where is Jim, where am I?" She attempted to pull her body up and release her foot, which felt like it was between the teeth of a ferocious animal. She hurt too much to be afraid. Something within her subconscious was sending alarm signals. Then it tumbled into her consciousness. I have fallen in the Clover Creek area.

Night sounds became increasingly louder, and she was all too aware of the fact that bears, javelinas, elk, deer and mountain lions resided on the Rim. Her greatest fear was that of mountain lions.

Sounds in darkness, she knew, were always louder than in daylight. She remembered that a full moon was expected. Where is the moon? Clouds obscured it, but occasionally it peeked through. There was a tiny backlight to the face of her wristwatch. Her glasses were still intact, tucked behind the headband hugging her ears. There had been a hat over the headband, but it had fallen off. She wore headbands to keep perspiration from running down her forehead when she sketched, and the hat to keep the sun from her face. The time on her watch appeared to be 10:20.

Jim's face repeatedly flashed before her. She cried as she considered the fact of the worry she knew he would experience. He had good reason to worry, and she condemned herself for the scrimpy note she had had left him, and the fact that she took an unnecessary chance in going by herself, with no one knowing where she was. Her son's face flashed before her, and she began to cry.

"Did he go through this in his accident before he died? Did he condemn himself for speeding? I hope he just prayed." Her heart, like a seed, cracked open, and prayers poured out. First came the promises, "I'll never do thus and so." Then came a depth of prayer. She reviewed in her mind her last steps and tried to calculate how far she was from the stone circle. It became irrelevant, as her foot was wedged. And she hurt.

Pray for wisdom. As her mind focused, action became necessary for her survival. She knew that energy flowed through her, as it flowed through all others. "Focus, focus."

Her hands were on her trapped foot, untying her boot. She loosened the shoestrings and, with a grunt, began prying her injured foot out of the shoe. She kept her sounds as constrained as possible. She didn't want to attract animals. Her fear barometer skyrocketed. Again, her prayer was: "Wisdom, wisdom." She knew that her focus must be on action. She tried diligently to control her fear. She tugged repeatedly, and finally her boot released her foot. The pain was excruciating, but she was free.

"Wisdom, wisdom," she whispered. The moon peeked out and seemed to light a trail for her.

Dragging her foot she crawled into a cave-like space between boulders. Boulders were above her and on either side. The moon, when it appeared, shone down on her between open spaces. She was wet. Rain was falling, and she moved closer to the interior. In a strange way, she was glad it was raining, as the rain would erase her scent if animals were hunting in the vicinity. As her comfort level minimally decreased, her pain throbbed.

Prayer brought a degree of comfort to her.

She reminded herself of silly Ann and the fact that she often said to be grateful for everything.

What would Ann say now? Tears welled within her, and she sobbed. Her water, along with everything, was back at the stone circle.

"I'm a fool," she exclaimed, and the tears poured.

The words, "No I'm not," came from within her. "I'm an explorer. There are worse places to die." It had dawned on her that she could die there. Jim was all she could think of.

"Did I write on the note, 'I love you?' Did I?" She felt herself fading from consciousness.

"Wisdom, wisdom," she whispered, as, again, she lost consciousness.

18 RUSTLING

*H*er body racked with pain, Jo pulled herself up on her right elbow. Again, she asked, "Where am I? Where is Jim?" Then she remembered. "Wisdom! Wisdom!" She was startled and terrified by a rustling outside the opening of her self-designed rock cave. She began picking up smaller stones to wall herself in. She kept a couple back in the event she might need to defend herself. Her hands were strong, and she reasoned that she could whop whatever several times, if necessary.

If I go down, it will be with a fight. The sound drew closer and became more quiet. With a medium-sized stone in hand, she became very still. In came a bird, dragging its leg. They stared at each other.

"Are you the same little fellow I was following when I got myself into this mess? Are you?"

In exhaustion, the drenched bird flopped on the ground near Jo.

The rain came down more heavily. Jo was thirsty, and she cupped both hands and stretched her arms outside the cave to catch rainwater. She was able to get a gulp from her cupped, very dirty hands. The rain trickled down the inside of her cave and a puddle formed on the dirt floor. The bird drank from the puddle. Jo considered the two of them to be unlikely cave mates. The bird provided a bit of a diversion for Jo, and she wondered what she provided for the bird. Her mind floated in and out of consciousness.

On one occasion, she was either hallucinating or experiencing a parallel universe. Jo had read of people who, through a focus of their consciousness, could propel themselves into an alternate universe. In her normal life, she wouldn't accept or reject such things. Such thoughts were not a part of her everyday world. In her present situation, she was desperate.

The bird merely watched her. She wanted to pet or hold it, but she dared not, for fear of scaring him away. Perhaps the bird was a she. Maybe it was an eagle.

"I think I will call you Wisdom. We're both injured, little buddy. Want to try finding a parallel universe with me?"

The bird blinked.

Jo began praying the "Our Father" and the "Hail Mary," both prayers she had learned as a child in Catholic schools. Many images flashed before her—pictures of her deceased parents, her son, siblings and her former husband.

"It's like a parade in here," she said to Wisdom.

Wisdom appeared to be asleep.

"Okay, little buddy, you went on without me. Focus, Jo, focus." She began deep breathing, and the pain began to subside somewhat.

"Focus, Jo, focus." She felt the slowing of her heart rate.

Again, she spoke aloud: "They say that unfocused energy fizzles. Little buddy, we are pure energy. Let's feel it and focus it forward. If only I could feel the movement!"

Maybe it was a dream; maybe not. She became smaller, and the bird became larger. Both exited through the rocks, which had become porous. The bird, Wisdom, carried Jo on his back. They soared upward. It occurred in the blink of an eye. Jo saw the stars and touched the full moon. And as quickly as they ascended, they descended and were back in the cave.

Jo found the experience to be freaky, and it frightened her. "It's entertaining, like watching TV, and I'm transported somewhere" Jo began crying again.

"Pray, Jo, pray." She looked at her watch. It appeared to be 3:10 a.m. Sunrise, she knew, would be at about 5:30 a.m. Surely they will be here. A narrow stream flowed through the cave, and Jo cupped her hands together and drank. "It looks clean, and you're drinking it."

She began a prayer: "Our Father Who art in heaven."

Prayer calmed her, and she felt it was grace. She gave thanks for grace, for wisdom, for the bird, Wisdom, and for rocks of her cave that kept her dry.

What? How can I give thanks for rocks? They almost killed me.

Wisdom stared at her.

"You're right, I did it. I was careless. Something I'm learning here, aren't I?" Nothing happens by accident, they say. "What the hell is this? I hurt. I don't deserve this."

Pray, pray, welled up from within her. "Hail, Mary, full of grace, the Lord is with thee...."

She experienced calmness. She picked up a rock and attempted to carve letters into the stone, but the rock disintegrated.

"Wisdom, if I die, I want to make sure Jim knows how I feel." She thought of her son and the agony she went through when she learned he died. What would she say to Jim? Through telepathy, perhaps Jim would know her thoughts.

She began talking aloud, and Wisdom slept.

"Dear Jim: It says 4:30 a.m. on my watch. I can't believe I let myself get here. I feel foolish, but, more than that, I'm terrified. I might die. And, truthfully, dying is an easier thought than the thought of having to leave you. You are the best thing I have let into my life. All those little quarrels don't matter now. Those passive aggressive behaviors I used took me off center. Love stands stronger. I see that now. All I can feel and see is your love. Please know that mine is always there for you. I'm stubborn enough that, if I die, I'll still be with you. But I would want you to find love again. What an interesting perspective to see things from this point. If I get out of this, I'm going to appreciate everything so much more."

Wisdom rustled about, and both of them heard coyotes in the distance. Several of them were howling, as they do when they surround a kill. Her vulnerability ever prevalent, she tried to focus on and calm Wisdom. His stare calmed her.

She focused her words on her new buddy, Wisdom.

"You have some strength in you. This is how you all live all the time, in the wild. Your eyes show no fear. How do you stay so centered?" She was freezing and had been shaking all night, perhaps as a result of her injury, but essentially because of the cold. She knew that desert nights could be as much as 30 to 40 degrees colder than daytime, especially in stormy weather.

"What am I going to say to God, to Jesus, when I meet them? And how could I forget my guardian angels. Somebody looked over us, little buddy. I didn't have to drag myself far to this cave. I could have been left in the open.

We're somewhat dry, and we're breathing."

Jo was in pain, but somehow something deeper was going on. She thought of Christ and His suffering on the cross. How did he do it, and why? He could have called upon legions of angels at any moment. Yet, through the pain he resurrected. Would He have resurrected without suffering pain? Would humans have noticed His resurrection without His suffering? Can we resurrect without pain, or can we notice our resurrections without pain? Wow, I don't know."

A glow seemed to appear in a far corner of the stone cave. Jo thought perhaps it was a hallucination, or maybe the rising of the sun. It hurt too much to move. As she watched, it appeared to become brighter. She thought of her son, dead those twenty years. She thought, too, of the song "Tears in Heaven," and she hummed the tune.

"Would you know my name if I saw you again?" She thought of the joy that would be hers if she could be with her son again. But, somehow, she knew she wasn't dying, but was only hurt. She thought of the possibility that her son might be able to go between parallel universes, and that the little light was a visit. She smiled. God's unconditional love for her was that same love that sees only love. She felt like that herself when she thought she might die. That kind of love stands, and everything else fades away. Anything other than love cannot stand alone for long. It has no real power. Her unconditional love for her son and for Jim was minuscule compared to the unconditional love of God for her. God's unconditional love for us, for His Son, for "all that is, was alive and well during the suffering of Christ." She focused on the little light.

"I love you." The light flickered and dissipated. She thought of God's love for her and that "He so loved the world that He sent His only Son." She thought of the Trinity; the Father, the Son and the Holy Spirit.

"Come, Holy Spirit, in the name of Jesus. Come, Holy Spirit, in the name of Jesus." She had learned that from Dr. Nemeh in one of his workshops.

"Come, Holy Spirit, in the name of Jesus. Dear God, help me." She faded into sleep.

19 SEARCH AND RESCUE

*T*he first calls to the sheriff's office came at about 3 o'clock in the wee hours of July 14. The note Jo left stated that she would be home by dark. The first reports were of a missing woman, with no indication as to where she might have gone. Most police will not consider someone missing until they have been gone 24 hours.

But, in the village of Pine, where Jo and Jim were well known, it was obvious to everyone that Jo had left for a day trip. A sheriff's deputy went to the house. Jo's license plate number, car model, etc., were all recorded. Within a couple of hours, a call came in from the field that her car had been located.

"Her car is of Highway 87, in brush, at the foot of Forest Route 142." It was also reported that the car was locked and nothing appeared out of place. She was not found in the immediate area.

Jim had the RV ready to go. When the call came, his hunting buddies started a chain of calls. Many people headed to Forest Road 142. Jim was on the phone with Bob, who remained calm.

"I'm two blocks from your house," Bob said. "Let me drive you in the RV."

"You're a good man, Bob. Please hurry". Both phones clicked off.

Within minutes, the two men were on their way to Forest Route 142. Search and Rescue had been notified, and volunteers were assembling as they drove. Search and Rescue from Strawberry, Payson and Pine were all helping. The hour was almost 5 a.m. In dry weather, Search and Rescue used low lights in the darkness to identify foot prints. The rainstorm would delay the rescue until they had visibility. The safety of rescue workers could not be compromised.

Bob pulled off 87 onto Forest Road 142. Through the rhythmic movement of the windshield wipers, they watched daylight as it broke over the horizon. Bob was grateful for daylight. Jim would never have understood waiting.

Jim's hands moved rapidly as he pointed. "There's her car! There's her car!"

Bob turned to him. "Let's see how far we can get this old Bessie up the hill."

Jim was intent as Bob drove, and he appeared anxious as the RV struggled up the hill.

"She can do it," Bob said. "We're better of parking at the top of this hill. We'll be central, and teams will probably head north, east, west and south."

Jim began crying uncontrollably. "I can't believe we're looking for my Jo, that she's missing. God, help me! Is that Ann over there?"

"Yeah, we had coffee earlier, way earlier."

"Wasn't she in California?"

"She got back last night, and was up at about four this morning. I went to her house to tell her about Jo, but she was gone. She was at the Early Bird Cafe. Before you called, I caught her there and gave her the news. She's here to support you, you know."

"She was quicker than us in getting here," Jim said.

"She didn't have to pull a Bessie."

Ann moved to Jim's window with a smile. "Everything will be okay."

Jim got out of the vehicle and hugged Ann. "I'm so scared."

"We're going to find her. Have faith."

The three walked arm in arm to the point where the Search and Rescue people had gathered. Jim's hunting friends were also there. People were teaming up, and each team had a map. No one stopped to talk to Jim. Everyone was focused on searching.

The team captain waved the trio over. Here's the central map. All routes are covered. Here's a map, and a walkie-talkie for you, Jim.

Bob can show you how to use it. We'll keep you updated. We'll find her."

Jim looked hopeful; the most hopeful Bob had seen him look since the ordeal began.

Jim pointed. "Look, there's Lev's car. Everyone is helping. He was supposed to work for me today. I called him, and I must have told him where they found Jo's car."

Someone in the background, one of Jim's hunting buddies overheard the conversation. "Let's hope he's not out here sabotaging the water supply."

Jim exploded. "Lev is a good man!"

Bob nodded in the affirmative and ushered Jim up the path. "We all know that, Jim."

The three continued up the road, as Bob surveyed the map. "Let's veer to the right and start on the trailhead toward West Clear Creek."

The assigned teams were just ahead, with two teams on ATVs. They all knew that the West Clear Creek team would have to dismount to get through the gate. The trail was intentionally designed to prohibit ATVs. Having ATVs parked outside the gate would allow for a quick exit and movement to the next destination.

20 LEV'S DAY ON JULY 14

*L*ev was heartbroken after speaking to his mentor, Jim, that Saturday morning and hearing the news about Jo. He wished he could take Jim's pain away. Lev had made his own life difficult, with his drinking habit. He had made many mistakes, especially that which resulted in his being fired from his job. His personal relationships were all damaged, and now he could add to the list of negatives that of having been accused of sabotaging the water system. His relationship with Jim was the first solid one of his life. When his job for Jim had canceled that morning, and Jim told him why, Lev felt depressed. He was tempted to drink; however, he went instead to The Early Bird for the $3.99 breakfast special. Many people in Pine were early-to-bed and early-to-rise, thus the place could be quite crowded in the wee hours.

At breakfast, he decided he would talk to no one, and would just head out on Highway 87 and look for Jo's car. He had to help Jim. With no information as to where Jo went, intuitively, he turned north on Highway 87. He had surmised her car would be near the road, as she was not an off-roader. Clint's Well was his original destination. His instinct paid off. Just past mile marker 285, he saw a Highway Patrol car at the side of the road. Behind the patrol car, he saw Jo's car. He knew the area well, and he turned off. He parked at the top of the hill and began looking for any indication of the direction

Jo had traveled. Obviously, it had rained the previous night, and rain was falling again. Any footprints would be washed away. To the right was the parking lot and the entrance to the West Clear Creek trailhead, a popular hiking area and a place for geo caching.

Before going through the gate at the trailhead, Lev glanced back and wondered if he should check in with the central gathering. They hadn't begun when he parked his car. He knew there was a search and rescue in progress, and that they never waste any time. He decided to go through the gate and remain focused on finding Jo. Knowing she was a sketch artist, he looked at the trail offerings as though through her eyes.

"What would attract her? What would she want to sketch?" He arrived at the cement and brick bridge. "Yes, this is it. I'll bet she came this way." He looked around for anything, a piece of trash, including a water bottle. He found nothing. He knew Jo would not intentionally leave trash. Then he heard a crunching sound beneath his boot. It was a piece of charcoal. He picked up the larger of the two intact pieces, turning it repeatedly in his hand. "Maybe, she draws with stuff like this, but it could also be from a previous campfire in the area." He threw it back on the ground. It wasn't sufficient evidence to prove she had been there.

He continued down the trail. It took him longer than it normally would because he poked and prodded while looking up and down the cliffs of rocks and trees. His step quickened as he approached the stone circle. He had seen it as a child and had heard it was made by campers. At his left was a strange pile of something within the circle.

"Bull's eye! It's Jo's art stuff." He reached for his whistle and began blowing. The sketch pad was wet and disintegrating. Something had pulled at her backpack, perhaps in the night, and the contents were scattered. Worry filled his mind.

"Jo! Jo!" While calling her name and blowing his whistle, he continued down the trail. His concern for her safety grew as he approached the boulder areas. On both sides of the creek were boulders, and only the most experienced hikers would continue on the path to West Clear Creek.

One hundred feet into the boulder area, Lev heard groaning. He continued whistling as he backtracked somewhat. He stood for a moment, listening. Then he saw a human hand reach out between rocks. He easily moved the rocks

that provided a cave. "Jo! Jo!"

They made eye contact.

"It's going to be okay, Jo. It's Lev. I'm here to help you."

He reached into his pack and handed a bottle of water to her.

"I know it's you, Lev. I thought I was dreaming."

"Don't move. Jim is on the other side." Lev reached for his whistle and aimed it toward the trailhead. He continued to calm her.

"I'm right here, Jo. I'm blowing the whistle to let them know you're here. Lev wished he had a walkie-talkie, but he felt help would be there soon.

Jo attempted to lift her head, and could barely do so. "Is Jim out there? Is he mad at me?"

"He loves you." Lev continued to blow the whistle, an ear-piercing sound that clearly bothered Jo. He reached down and held her hand. "Everything will be all right, Jo."

Jo appeared ready to vomit. "Where's Wisdom? Wisdom!" she called.

"What do you mean?" Lev thought she was hallucinating. Jo was clearly upset, and she tried to get up. "Wisdom, my eagle friend!

Where is she?"

"Stay still, Jo." He held her hand. "We'll look when the others get here. Just relax and try to remain calm. He saw that her ankle was badly injured, and he wondered how she managed to build an enclosure, and how she got inside. He stepped outside again and continued blowing the whistle. Then, he got a response.

"Jo, help is here. Hang tight." He moved quickly toward the stone circle and began seeing heads as they bobbed up and down. And they saw him.

He let the whistle fall from his lips. "Over here, down the side about 100 feet. She's conscious, and in pain. It looks like a broken ankle." Lev led the way, as walkie-talkies crackled with the good news.

Jo was soon surrounded by caring people. Quietly, she grasped Lev's hand. "Find Wisdom."

The medical people were focused on her foot and the goose egg-size bump on her head.

"Was someone with you?" a rescuer asked. "Who is Wisdom?"

"A bird," Jo feebly replied. "An eagle, I think."

"I'm looking," Lev whispered in her ear. He stepped away from the circle. He then believed her.

Walkie-talkies crackled again, and Jim shouted above them.

Jo heard him, and she mustered all the strength possible.

"Honey, I'm so sorry."

"Never mind! How are you doing? Let them help you."

"I have so much to tell you."

"We can talk later. I'm almost to you. We're on the trail.

Bob, Ann and I are almost to you. Love you."

"Love you more."

"Lev found me, and now he's looking for Wisdom, my bird." Jo screamed in pain as they prepared to move her injured foot. They were able to administer pain medication, but were most concerned about the injury to her head.

She gave the team all the information she could remember as to how and when she made decisions that took her to Clover Creek. "Thank you all so much. I could be dead, if it weren't for you. How can I thank you?" She was tired and appeared to be losing consciousness.

As Jim arrived, he found Jo's head in a brace. He grasped her hand, and both cried.

"Arrangements have been made to transport you by helicopter," he said, but you have to be moved to a flat area.

A transport gurney appeared, and everyone moved to the assigned location of a makeshift helicopter pad. No one noticed that Lev had quietly slipped away. He continued down the boulder trail in search of Wisdom.

Bob and Ann returned to the stone circle and gathered Jo's belongings. With no room for Jim in the helicopter, he hurried down the trail and was whisked away by an ATV to a waiting car and a fast trip to the hospital. Bob would drive Jim's RV home. As they approached the central location of the search, both were surprised to see the number of people involved in the rescue.

The search director thanked everyone. "We had over a hundred of you fine folks helping in this search. As you may have heard, Jo was found near Clover Creek on the West Clear Creek Trail. Her injuries are not fully known. It appears she has a broken ankle and a lump the size of an egg on her forehead. She's on the way to the hospital by helicopter Thank you, all. I can't express my appreciation enough."

The search director continued "May this serve as a reminder for all of us. Please, please, tell someone where you're going, and don't hike alone. That's all. Again, thank you. Job well done. If you were using our walkie-talkies, or any of our supplies, please hand them to me. Let's all go home."

Everyone applauded. Then, the air was filled with the sound of goodbyes and of car doors slamming.

21 BOB AND ANN LEAVE CLOVER CREEK

*B*ob and Ann walked arm in arm to Jim's RV, and Bob placed Jo's belongings inside.

"Ann, do you want to meet me at their house. We can unload Jo's belongings, and I can park the RV. Then, if you'll drive me back up here, I can pick up Jo's car and take it to their house."

"That'll work. I still can't believe they found her so soon." A hunting friend of Jim's approached them, with his hand outstretched. "I'm Billy. You may not remember me, but I'm an old friend of Jim's. I can drive one of their vehicles home; either the RV or her car, if you have the keys. You know, Jim was at my party, and I feel so guilty. I was encouraging him to spend the night so that he could drink with us."

Bob had his hand in Jo's pack and retrieved her car keys.

"Those things happen. Jim would be the first to tell you not to feel guilty. Jo is okay. Billy, if you can help, that would be great. We'll give you a ride back here to get your car."

"Actually, my wife is over there, and she'll follow." Billy pointed to an SUV. We live at Forest Lakes, so we'll head home after I deliver Jo's car. I'm glad for a happy ending."

Ann finished shaking his hand. "We are too."

"Our hunting buddies are at the hospital, or on their way, so we'll check in with them when we hit Payson. Who knows, we may decide to stay a night or two."

They hugged one another. Billy waved to his wife, indicating he had Jo's keys and would drive her car to the house.

Billy's wife waved, shaking her head in the affirmative.

She called out the window, "I'll meet you all at their house."

Ann walked to her car, and Bob started the engine of the RV. In a procession, of sorts, all headed to Jim and Jo's house. On the way toward Highway 87, both Bob and Ann noticed Lev's car was still there. Each made a mental note to mention it to the other.

About half an hour later, the RV was in its spot at their house and Jo's car was in the garage. Billy, along with his wife, was heading down the road to Payson. Bob's vehicle had been at Jim and Jo's all morning. Ann had pulled behind Bob's car. Both unloaded Jo's art supplies and everything else had been put in the RV, such as water, snacks, etc. Bob opened the door to the back deck, to let in fresh air.

"It's too early for a glass of wine. Want a coke?" Bob held open the refrigerator door. "There's some sandwich meat. Are you hungry?"

"Not really. I had breakfast. You only had coffee."

Bob was squirting mustard on a bun. "Want some chips?

Ann rummaged through the refrigerator. "And here is some salsa."

Bob shook his head in the affirmative.

The sun was shining on the uncovered back deck, and they headed to the sheltered front porch. It was not yet noon, but they had spent a full day. A large wooden swing stood at an end of the porch, with small tables on either side. Bob finished his sandwich in record time, while Ann had chips with salsa.

"This salsa is good," Bob commented. "It's from the grocery store, and it's freshly made in Pine. Hey, did you notice that Lev's car was still in the lot?"

Ann swallowed a chip. "Yeah, I did. It's cool that he's the one who found her. Maybe the town will lighten up. I wonder why he stayed behind?"

Bob shook his head, indicating he didn't know. "Back on the trail, when we all got the news that she was found, they gave the walkie-talkie to Jim. I could hear a lot of the conversation. I heard something about an eagle. Go find her eagle. Did you hear anything like that?"

I was farther behind," Ann said. "I didn't hear much. Are there eagles up there?"

"Yes, in Dry Lake, so it would be natural to spot one near Clover Creek. But find one on the ground? I don't know."

"Maybe Lev wanted to hike," Ann suggested.

"He was there to help find Jo, and he did just that. The man deserves credit for being a caring man."

22 JO, RECUPERATING AT HOME, TALKS WITH ANN

*J*o was released from the hospital after two nights, and it had been a couple of weeks since her ordeal at Clover Creek. Her foot was fractured, and she suffered a mild concussion. Jim was overly protective, and Jo was content in being nurtured at home.

Jo let Ann in through the front door. "I'm so glad you could come over today, Ann. I would have been fine alone, though."

"But I wanted to visit with you. I was waiting for the right opportunity. This is it."

"Jim probably thinks I'll take off again. Maybe he disabled the car."

Both women laughed.

Jim overheard the women from the kitchen, and he joined them.

"Hey, that's a great idea, Jo. Thanks, my little love." He had a briefcase in hand, and he bent to kiss her. "Goodbye, my love."

Jim hugged Ann. "I Love you, too. Bye, Ann I'm so glad it worked out for you to come over today. I'll be back in a few hours."

Ann smiled. "Take your time, Jim. Jo and I have a lot to talk about."

Jo piped in. "And it would bore you. So, get out of here." Both women laughed as the door closed and Jim was gone.

Jo led the way to the kitchen. "Ann, help yourself to coffee, donuts, whatever you see in there. Just help yourself. I want to sit on the back deck, if it's okay with you."

"Sure, it's a beautiful day. Do you need anything, Jo?"

"No, thanks. We have a routine here. Jim fills my coffee thermos and plops fresh bread from the bakery on the deck table, along with preserves from the Honey Store. I know how to live, you know."

"Isn't it great? You and Jim have it all worked out."

"Speaking of men, what's going on with you and Bob? You seem like a perfect match for each other."

"We are definitely moving in a new direction."

"What do you mean? Did you have sex? I'm being too bold. Since my venture in the wilderness, I hold nothing back. Could be a curse."

"None of your business! And, yes, you are being bold. It's okay, though. We're friends. If I should need advice, I might even come to you."

"I apologize for my mouth. It was intrusive. I know what it's like, dating, and all that. You two seem to be friends."

Ann's expression softened. "That, we are. And it makes the getting-to-know-each-other phase so much easier. Sex is a new element and well, we're seniors."

Jo smiled. "Jim always said it was up to me when. Damn, he's a good kisser! And he's a kind man."

Ann took a sip of her drink. "Bob initially thought I was a man-hater because I've been divorced so long."

Jo looked surprised. "How long?"

Ann continued. "About 20 years. All divorces are hard on people. For me, it was the death of a dream. My dream was tied to my former husband. I must have been obsessed." She appeared amused. "Now, I'm so glad he's gone. He was a womanizer. Actually, he was my best teacher of what love isn't."

Jo nodded her head. "I know what you mean. I get it, it's hard to explain. I appreciate Jim so much. I know what a great guy he is. If I had met him years earlier, I might not have paid attention to him."

"So," Ann began, "Bob and I are taking it slow. Neither of us is dating anyone else. He's comfortable, like a favorite pair of shoes."

Both women refilled their coffee cups from Jo's thermos.

"Bob appreciates my icons, but he thinks

some of my work, such as Mystic Rib and Mother Eve, are feminist."

"Feminist? What does he mean by that?"

"My interpretation is that he means powerful women. Both the masculine and the feminine are within each of us. It's the blending of the two, much like sex. Sex is a communion of spirit and body. He's getting it that it's the two within the one. Like, I'm learning the blend of the feminine within Jesus. Jesus was wholly human, both feminine and masculine, as well as both divine and human."

Jo laughed. "Just mention sex, and I bet Bob will buy it."

Both women chuckled.

"Bob is a deep thinker. Enough of us, Jo. How are you feeling? Any pain?"

"No pain. In fact, inside, I am great. My soul, you know, felt that communion you're talking about. When I realized I was in trouble on the trail, I could hear your voice, telling me to be grateful for everything."

Ann was silent, listening intently as Jo continued.

"It's much like our conversation about the mean men in our prior lives. They showed us what we don't want and made it easy to see the beauty of these good men in our present lives."

"Not everybody learns that way. Some women know goodness and reject anything less. You and I learned the other way. Although it may have been the hard way, I'm glad I learned. I wouldn't trade it for anything, would you?"

"No way! I have heaven on earth now, with Jim. Actually, I have it with or without Jim. My relationship with God and with Jesus is more powerful."

Ann loved the thought, heaven on earth. It made her think of Eve.

Jo held Ann's hand. "Oh, Ann, my friend! I have to tell about my experience out there. This broken ankle and my concussion are nothing."

"Take your time, Jo. I have all afternoon."

"Jim scoffs at me when I talk about spirituality," Jo began. "I'll read to you what I wrote when I returned home."

Jo read aloud to Ann:

"I learned that God's love is unconditional. Whatever I do, God loves me. It's difficult to translate that love into human terms. We humans love to judge, and I tell myself not to judge the judgment of others. That, too, is judging. Remember to be love.

Like in Eden, I can choose the effect or choose God. Surrender all of me to God. It can't be piecemeal. If there is any fragment of me withdrawing, I am not whole, therefore, I can't surrender my all.

The tree in the garden was a tree of the knowledge of both good and evil. Not two trees, but one. In choosing the apple, it was both sides, good and evil. Like a coin with two sides, I can't just choose one side in choosing the coin. I can focus on one side, but the coin exists. Return to the garden, Jo, and get out of the effect. Be with God. Let go all coins, or rather, all effects. This time, I know I'm choosing God. Thoughts are distractions, like pain and fear, and can take my eye off God. God is the isness.

I have the free will to choose God or something else. If I think I have to be responsible for an adult someone else, that would make me their god. It would put me into effect and co-dependency. I am not responsible for another. Choose God. I decide. If I surrender, there is nothing to decide or think about. I AM. Don't judge judgment. Just allow. Don't ignore or deny, as that gives power to what is being ignored or denied. That is all ego. Observe, allow and choose effect, or choose God. Surrender. Surrender. I did, and I do.

There is consciousness while I am in a human body.

There is another consciousness that extends far beyond the body and doesn't have its origin in the body. I think it would best be called energy. The consciousness that extends around me got me through my ordeal. It wasn't my regular consciousness. I moved away from thought and chose God. Thought takes away from choosing God. Thoughts can be ego's distraction. Just be.

And that, my dear Ann, is the story of my resurrection." Both women sat in silence. Jo's words echoed Ann's journaling with Eve.

Jo was the first to speak. "Those are my notes, Ann. Any comment? Too weird, or too wacky? Something happened to me up there. I can't deny it."

"Nothing to add," Ann replied. "Is there another sheet under that paper?"

"I wasn't going to read it, but I will. It's just that when I was in the hospital and they were checking for brain injury, they were so curious about my eagle story. My sense is that they think it was a hallucination. It wasn't, Ann. I promise."

"I believe you. Read it, if you're comfortable doing so."

"Okay, Ann. I called the little eagle Wisdom. Truthfully, it was he, or she, that I was following when I fell. It was so unusual, the rock circle, and then this little eagle. He didn't belong there, I thought, and his wing, or his leg, appeared injured. He looked at me as though he knew me."

Ann listened intently. "Maybe he did."

"Thanks." A tear rolled down Jo's cheek, and she patted Ann's hand.

"His face was striped, with a luminous white. He was beautiful. What I did was stupid. Then, after I fell, and regained consciousness, there he was again. My ankle didn't hurt at first, but then it was excruciating. The idea came to me to crawl under rocks and barricade myself in. Then, there was the little bird again. He barricaded in with me. He never made a noise, but he read my thoughts."

Jo picked up the sheet she had hidden under her other writing:

"Dear Wisdom:

Who are you? I know you are of God.

Simply, you led me. I don't understand why I followed and allowed myself to get into such a dangerous situation. I do understand that what I learned is beyond measure. For the first time ever, in the silence, I felt an energy, or a vibration, surround me. Not a whirlwind, but like electricity on the verge of igniting all around me. Were you like a dove sent to guide me, like the Holy Spirit? In time, understanding will come to me. Know that I love you, my special little bird.

Love, Jo"

23 LEV SEARCHING FOR THE EAGLE

*L*ev was a man with the ability to see with the physical eye and the courage to see beyond the physical. During his time with AA, he learned about the Power greater than himself. Many things had been revealed to him by the other AA participants. He wasn't afraid to make his own path. He knew he was powerless over alcohol, but he had power in his choices, all his choices. Even though he didn't understand what Jo had said about a bird, or an eagle, he was willing to believe her. Besides, he enjoyed being in nature, and it was a beautiful morning to be hiking. Jo was on her way to the hospital. As crazy as it sounded to him, looking for Jo's eagle was the least he could do.

The rain the previous night had washed the leaves on the trees, leaving a vibrant green. They shone in the sunlight. He could imagine Jo's fear, and he was grateful for the beauty of the moment and the knowledge that she was safe. He found joy in having found her. He loved Jim, and, by virtue of his relationship with Jim, he loved Jo. Jo had been his Sunday school teacher many years before.

As he moved along the creek, Lev hummed nondescript music, always with his eyes wide open and searching. Within 300 feet, he came upon an eagle feather. It was hard to tell how long it had been there, but he thought of it as a sign. He wanted more than anything to prove Jo right. A few hundred feet beyond, he found another small feather, that may, or may not, have been from an eagle. The view became increasingly more beautiful with each turn. A large boulder jutted over the creek.

A perfect place to pray. I guess any place is a perfect place to pray, but it's so much easier when it's steeped in beauty.

He climbed to the top of the rock and became silent.

He always felt that silence was the language of God. True communion with God was in silence. Allowing the energy to enfold and surround him, he nestled closer against the rock. With eyes closed, he became aware of his breath, which seemed to inhale peace and exhale wisdom.

How interesting, Lev thought. I chose the word wisdom for my exhale, and Jo named her bird Wisdom. Coincidence. He experienced peace. A rustling in the brush brought his attention to his physical surrounding. On the other side of the creek, 100 feet away, appeared a bird rustling in the brush.

"Little fellow, are you Jo's friend?" Lev felt foolish. But, heck, who's going to hear me, well, other than God.

The bird was moving about under the brush. It was hard for Lev to get a good look. But he could tell Jo he saw a bird near her site, and that it appeared to have an injury. Lev continued his private prayer. The entire area seemed to fall into silence. Not even a trickle could be heard from the creek.

Upon completion of his prayer, Lev opened his eyes.

On the highest cliff, overlooking the canyon was an eagle. Lev had no idea how long he had been in prayer. He was speechless. As quickly as he opened his eyes, the eagle spread his wings and became airborne. Lev had never been so close to an eagle. He questioned his eyesight, but decided it didn't matter. He recognized the fact that the eagle had always been known as a source of power. One of Lev's buddies in AA, who was from Alaska, had told about his native people. The natives believed that Noah's Ark was about an eagle that took the animals, two by two, onto his wings and flew them to safety. Lev was happy and felt blessed to be part of the adventure. When the time was right, he would share his experience with Jo, and only Jo. He said a prayer of thanksgiving, turned around, and headed for his car. He was almost grateful, that he was an alcoholic. Otherwise, he might not have experienced the depth of prayer and felt the energy. He wished he could have learned prayer in a different way, but it was alcoholism that led him to God. It didn't matter how, only that he had found God. Lev was learning the meaning of contentment.

He made his way out of the canyon. In his ascent he became aware of loud noises to his right, on the dirt road above him. Hikers, he thought, but their sounds and energy sounded loud. Some of the language he did not understand, and he wondered if it might be a foreign language. The hair on the back of his neck stood up. Lev was very aware of the water systems throughout the area. A major well was down the road a short distance and across the main highway. He also knew that it was well patrolled, with cameras on site. Homeland Security was present in Pine. There were problems with the water earlier in the summer and bottled water had been distributed to each house. His cousin, Stu, had helped with the distribution. Lev knew that many people thought he, Lev, had sabotaged the system. Lev knew the truth about himself and was 100 percent sure that management missed the clues that water was short in the system. They had run out of water, and corrosion from the dirty old pipes had fallen into the water. He didn't believe that sabotage had been committed. He was the one blamed, however, by some people. He had been fired for drunken driving, and he accepted responsibility. He was glad for the mandated counseling that led to AA. He knew the new water system was good. The new wells went down 1,000 to 1,200 feet for water, instead of the previous 500 feet. Rumors implicated him as a disgruntled former employee. He waited in the trees and brush on the trail for the foreign sounds to decrease and disappear. When all was clear he continued his path, directly to his car, and didn't look back. There was a lot of riparian work going on in the area, and the people may have been foreign students or with some sort of information exchange.

24 LEV AND JO

Several weeks after the Clover Creek rescue, Jim had hired Lev to do yard work. It was the first opportunity for Jo to spend time alone time with Lev.

Lev was finishing the yard work, when Jo called out to him. "Lev, come in for some fresh iced tea when you want a break."

"I'm almost finished. Can you give me 10 minutes?"

"Sure, I'm just reading the paper. It's looking good out there. Jim will be so pleased when he gets back tonight." Jo was positive that Jim had hired Lev to look after her, under the pretense of cleaning the yard. It didn't matter, as she was glad to spend some private time with him. In her mind, she could still feel the comfort of seeing him and touching his hand as he rescued her. She wondered what gibberish had come out of her mouth. It was all a blur.

Lev knocked on the back screen door. "Do you still have tea for me?" He removed his cap and wiped his feet as Jo opened the door.

"Come in and sit a spell." She had placed a plate of homemade oatmeal cookies on the tray beside a pitcher of iced tea, with fresh lemons and oranges floating on top. Lev took a seat at the kitchen table.

Jo poured the tea. "I don't know that I ever got a chance to properly thank you for finding me."

"There was a whole army out there, I just happened to be first. It was something I'll never forget." Lev chose not to bring up the subject of the bird, or the name "Wisdom."

Jo sipped her tea. "You know, Lev, I believe I mentioned something about the little bird with me. Do you remember my having said anything?"

"Yes, m'am, I do."

"What did I say?"

"Just that he was injured and that he stayed with you. You seemed pretty worried about him. You were hurting, but you were more concerned about the bird."

"People probably thought I was nuts, but that's okay. You know, there was a bird?"

Lev smiled. "Yes, m'am, I do."

"My husband loves you. He says you're a thinker."

Lev grinned. "I respect your husband. He's a good man. You know, he thinks my bird story is goofy, and that it didn't happen."

"I know. You asked me to check on the bird. At first, I thought it was silly, but for you, I would do it. And everyone else was caught up in getting you safely out of there."

"Everyone was great."

"Search and Rescue is the best. There is only one helicopter for the state to use in rescue. The sheriff's office was able to authorize its use for your rescue."

"Only one?"

"Yeah, and it's based in Tucson. Everyone was so focused on your rescue, so I just quietly moved down the creek. I didn't expect to find much, and then, about a couple of hundred feet away, I found a feather, and then another."

"I'm surprised that you believed me. There was a bird, an eagle, and I called him Wisdom."

"After a mile or so, I sat on a rock and meditated. You know, the area where the boulders become increasingly larger, and finally there's the largest one?"

"Not really. I stop when it gets difficult. But please go on."

"On a boulder across the creek, in the low brush, was a vulture feasting on a fish. That in itself is odd. It didn't appear to be injured. Much later, and after my meditation, I swear a saw an eagle high on the cliff over me. I swear he stared at me. I was motionless. He seemed to glow. Then he lifted off. I didn't have a good view, but in the air he sure looked like an eagle

I think that little bird was my angel. He took my mind of my pain. He took my thoughts away."

"I'm sure your giving nurturing to the bird took your mind off your pain. Lev, do you believe in angels and spirits?"

"I believe in God."

The phone rang, and Jo excused herself.

Lev, feeling their conversation had ended, excused himself. "I'm off to my next job, Jo."

Jo hugged Lev and said goodbye. As she watched him leave, she reached for the telephone.

25 BOB AND LEV

*L*ev arrived to work at Bob's right on time. Bob had hired him to do handyman work. Hiring Lev was Bob's way of reaching out and keeping in touch with him. He genuinely liked Lev.

"Morning, Bob. Reporting for duty."

Bob returned the salute. "Grab a cup of coffee, if you
want."

Lev declined. "Here to work, man."

"Let's do it."

The men skipped small talk and worked for two hours clearing brush and piling it onto the front of a lot near the street. People in Pine keep track of hours spent cleaning their lots. They give their timesheet to the fire department, where the time is calculated for grant-writing purposes. The fire department picks up the burnable brush and carts it away for a bonfire. Bob almost declared it "Miller

Time," but he knew Lev didn't drink.

"Time to stop. Let's grab a sandwich and soda inside. If you've got time, we can sit on the deck and visit while we eat."

Lev nodded in the affirmative. "Sounds good to me. I have nothing else planned, except to clean my house."

Bob pulled out the cold cuts, bread, mustard and all the other sandwich ingredients. He pointed to the bottom shelf of soda pop and filled two glasses with ice.

"Pick your poison."

Lev chose a Sprite, and the men headed toward the deck. Bob decided to get to the point. "Did you hear anything about Homeland Security checking around up here?"

Lev looked surprised. "Not yet. What about? I mean, I know they all think something strange happened to the water pipes but I don't think so. There was a mechanical problem, and corrosion took a toll. That's all. I can't believe anyone thought I had anything to do with it. Do you?"

"No, I don't. If Homeland Security wanted information from you, they would have contacted you. The latest thing they're checking on now is up by Clover Creek, where you rescued Jo."

"I don't get it," Lev said. "What happened up there?

"When?"

"The day of the rescue there was suspicious activity caught on camera by the water hole. Nothing of consequence happened. It's more of who those unidentified people might be, and what they were doing there."

Lev took long sips of his drink. Bob continued.

After everyone cleared out, your car was the only one parked in the vicinity.

A light bulb appeared to go off in Lev's head. "Come to think of it, when I was leaving I heard people on the trail high above me, and I couldn't understand what they were saying. It may have been a foreign language. I just don't know."

"Why did you stay behind?"

Lev looked like a deer caught in headlights. He took his time to respond. "I just felt like being alone after all the commotion and I continued down the creek. The people I heard weren't anywhere near the creek bed. It was on my way out that I heard them. They never saw me."

"How do you know they didn't see you?"

"I hid in trees. Something wasn't right, though."

Bob hesitated before he spoke. "It doesn't make sense to

me that you would continue down the creek after you rescued Jo and everyone else was leaving. Granted, there was a lot of commotion, but I could see you, as the initial rescuer, being

the one carrying her out. You just disappeared."

"Bob, I swear I am not hiding anything." Lev gathered his wits. "This is going to sound crazy. When I first got to Jo, and even after, she kept talking about a bird being with her within the boulders. She even named the bird Wisdom. She kept pleading with me to find him, because the bird was injured."

Bob appeared surprised. "You know, when they passed the walkie-talkie to Jim, so he could speak to Jo, I heard something about a bird. Jo sounded hysterical, and most thought she was hallucinating."

"What do you think?"

"Truthfully Bob, within a couple hundred feet, I started finding feathers, first one feather and then another. May have been eagle feathers. It was weird."

"Did you tell Jo?"

"But that's not all. When I stopped and finished my meditation, I saw a bird take of high up, and it just may have been an eagle. He was so high, I wasn't sure."

"There are eagle nests in Dry Lake."

"Yeah, but this one wasn't injured. He stared me down, I swear. And then he flew off. Crazy huh?"

"Yeah, you're right, Lev, it sounds crazy, but it's a clearer explanation of why you went down the creek."

"Can you imagine me telling that to Homeland Security, especially if they think I had anything to do with sabotage?"

"Wow!"

"Jo asked me about it."

"What does she think?"

"She believes in angels and spirits. She thinks the bird was there to help her, and that, in some strange way, it did. She calls the whole day her day of resurrection"

"I guess, Lev, one has to ask who we are to judge."

"There's a lot I don't know, Bob. There aren't many people I would share this information with. It sounds bizarre but I have seen some strange things in my life. In AA, we call it our Higher Power."

"You know, Ann and I have gotten into some spiritual conversations. I'm laughing at your mention of AA."

Lev was perplexed.

"No, Lev, I'm not laughing at AA. It's just that she and I reference 'before' and 'after' the apple when we talk about Adam and Eve. You know, in the Garden of Eden. AA sounds like after the apple."

Lev laughed. "And I thought I might sound weird to you."

"This spiritual stuff means a lot. The older I get, the more I realize how little I know. When I was younger, I thought I was very masculine and strong."

"Me, too, Bob, especially when I drank. Now, I get the paradox, 'lose my life, gain my life.' I am powerless."

"I understand you now, Lev. But 20 years ago, no way."

"Life takes us in a circle."

"Ann is so into Eve, and, by osmosis, so am I. It started out a feminine thing, with Ann being an old feminist and all. Now, I realize it's the journey of all of us. Finding the oneness in duality. The two are one."

"What do you mean, Bob? I don't follow."

"I'll give it my best shot, but Ann is the one to speak with. Femininity is that part of our being that is sensitive, nurturing, intuitive and receptive to spirit. It's not the sex organs. By the same token, masculinity is strength, courage and endurance."

"Okay, keep going."

"When you have sex with another, there's a communion of spirit. When you love someone, it's beyond the physical. The two of you are in communion. As a man, I learn to tap into my feminine side, balancing it with my masculinity. I commune with spirit into the wholeness of my being. Separation is old stuff."

"Then, Bob, are you saying that ultimate communion is like sex with God?"

"Like I said, Lev, talk to Ann. You know, in French, the word for orgasm, I believe, means little death. Two-in-one. It's similar to the three-in-one, or trinity. We are all one."

"Why is it that we men always understand things in terms of sex? I do get it. If I'm integrated, then all of me is free to be in communion with God. When I separate out, I lose communion. I do know there is a Higher Power in my life."

"Back to Homeland Security, they may or may not talk to you. All you can tell them is what you know. Skip the bird stuff, though."

"Truthfully, I do have a sense that all is well. I'm not sure if my meditation generated that feeling, or the presence of a Higher Power. Wisdom, how did Jo come up with that name?"

"You'll have to ask her. I'm going to Ann's for dinner tomorrow night. Who knows where our conversation will go."

Lev decided it was time to clean his house. "Talk to you later, Bob. Thanks for the job."

"Let me pay you. Hold on." Bob went into the house to retrieve his wallet.

Lev was more grateful than ever for his friendship with Bob. I now have two mentors, he thought, Jim and Bob, along with my sponsor and my fellow AA members.

And Bob was grateful for Lev. In some strange way,

Lev had taught him the importance of not judging. While Bob knew Lev was innocent of sabotage, it became irrelevant in comparison to the lesson he had learned about not judging. In Bob's opinion, judging Lev wasn't his business. Judgment would be the responsibility of a court of law, and of spiritual law. Bob considered the lesson concerning non-judgment as a personal resurrection.

Later that evening, Bob wrote the following, to be given to Lev:

LIFE IS LIKE A TAPESTRY

Life is like a tapestry.

One has to step away to enjoy the beauty.

It's a different picture up close.

A tapestry can't be cut into blocks or pieces.

The threads weave through the whole,

To complete the picture.

There are themes,

Like winter, spring summer and fall.

The yarns on my loom of life

Will be both different and the same

As the yarn on other looms.

What may look like a tangled mess to me,

May be the beginning of a masterpiece.

I may think I know how

To untangle another's loom,

But it would be like one tree

Trying to grow for another.

Only the Master Weaver sees the whole.

At times, I may be part of the untangling,

But only the Master Weaver sees the whole.

When I think I know something,

I realize I know nothing.

When I think I am separate,

I realize I am connected to all,

At the very core of my being.

What I thought was you and you and you,

Was me and me and me.

I am a piece of yarn

In the tapestry of humankind,

At the hand of the Master Weaver.

26 DINNER WITH ANN, BOB AND EVE

*B*ob arrived at Ann's home for dinner with a bottle of cabernet sauvignon, a bouquet of flowers and the play he had journaled concerning Adam and Eve. He was happy for the deepening aspect of their relationship, one in which he could be honest in being himself. It seemed eons since he had written about Adam and Eve.

His thoughts continued aloud: "What is it about love that makes it seem the whole world has changed? Imagine the magnitude if we just opened and received the love of God?"

Ann greeted him at the door. He entered awkwardly, with flowers and his journal in one hand and a bottle in the other.

Both laughed as Chopper barked for attention.

Bob embraced Ann. "This feels good, Ann."

Ann beamed in happiness. "I'm so glad we're friends."

Bob took a step back. "I hope this isn't your way of saying just friends."

"Friends first. Sex can mess things up if it isn't right."

"Heavens, Ann, we are old enough to know."

"Intimacy requires trust," Ann said.

"Let's drink to that."

They let go the embrace, and Bob patted Chopper. "How you doing, Chop?"

Ann took a vase from a cupboard and began arranging the flowers. "I'm doing a stir-fry. Make yourself at home."

"I should have brought white wine."

"I like what you brought. My cheese is a bit pungent, so that will go well. Hey, I have white wine. We can open both."

"That sounds good, red with the cheese and white with dinner."

"What's the book you brought?"

He popped the cork. "That, my dear, is a surprise for after dinner. I want to read to you."

"I'm intrigued. Do I have to wait?"

"Your wish is my command."

"They all say that in the beginning of a relationship."

"My, angel, Ann." He wanted to say 'my jaded angel,' but thought better of using the word "jaded."

He felt it was going to be a beautiful night.

They settled on the deck in their favorite

chairs, as Chopper curled up and chewed on his favorite bone.

"I want you to know, Ms. Ann, that I took seriously your request to think about Eve. Remember when I went up to the Butte tower?"

"Yeah, please continue, Mr. Bob."

"Out on the catwalk, in the midst of nature, I began my thoughts on Adam and Eve. It was strange, as though they were there. I wrote a play, just for fun. Truthfully, just for you, Ann."

"You channeled her? Not so strange, Bob. I think I did,

too. It's like someone is talking through me. I think it's more like an archetype of ancient Adam and Eve, like a dream. Everyone knows who Adam and Eve were. The question is, have we integrated them, are we in union?"

"I think I get what you're saying, not that I buy it. We conjure up this ancient view, and it comes through."

"Projection. Remember, Bob, years ago when people journaled their 'inner child?'"

"Sort of. Back in the '90s, everyone had an inner child

from their past that got stunted or repressed. And if one became child-like in his writing, they could heal the inner child. What they did was to integrate past pain instead of repressing it. And, in so doing, they became whole."

"Exactly, I've metaphorically placed my inner child on my lap and journaled. It's almost like multiple personalities, and we integrate into oneness."

"You're funny, Ann. We both sound crazy."

"You knew that before you came in the door. Seriously, I want to hear your play. Then I'll read my journaling."

"Better idea, let's swap. You read mine, and I'll read yours.

Later, after we've digested what each has written, we'll get together and philosophize."

"Better for another day, but I'm eager to read your play.

You're quite creative." They smiled at each other.

"You know, Ann, we are both weird, and it feels like there's an energy, a vibration in this room."

Ann cleared her throat. "Maybe it's a paradox. Seriously, everything of a spiritual nature leans toward paradox. We are neither spiritual nor human; we are both. A thousand years

from now, where will you and I be?"

Bob looked toward the sky. "Heaven, I hope. It's strange

that this writing is so cool. Not that I will ever do it again, but I know there's more to this life than my everyday living. And there's more to my everyday living than this physical life.

It's a paradox!"

"You're a wise man."

Bob's phone rang. It was Lev, and he sounded excited.

"Bob this is great! I wanted to let you know

that I got a job, not my same job, but a job with the water company. They're happy about my AA and are willing to start tabla rosa, whatever that means."

"Great! Tabla rosa means a clean slate. You're starting fresh."

"I figured. They said my record is cleared for non-driving jobs. They even had spoken to Homeland Security, and I'm 100 percent cleared. Apparently, Jim and Jo wrote a glorious letter of recommendation for me. I feel great. The weirdest thing, though, is that I'm going to help dig and foster a riparian area in Clover Creek. The area has drawn national attention. In fact, the day of Jo's rescue they had international visitors in the area."

"I'll bet those were the people you heard."

"Yeah, I think so. It's a whole new beginning for me. Just want to let you know and to thank you for having faith in me."

"It's an honor knowing you, my friend."

The men said their goodbyes, and Bob focused on Ann.

"That's pretty cool. Lev has a job and has been cleared by everyone to return to work."

Ann nodded in agreement. "He paid his dues for excessive drinking. I'm glad he's been given a second chance."

"I learned not to judge and to allow the Master Weaver to weave one's life. It's what they call 'turning it all over to God,' in AA. That's what I learned from Lev. Lev didn't need any resolving from humans. He needed God."

"He's the wounded healer." Ann looked at her watch.

"I'm going to start the wok. We have fresh veggies from

Dave's garden. Are you hungry for stir-fry?"

"I'm very hungry. Can I help?"

"It's easy. Do you want to eat outside?"

Dinner ran late, and afterward both Ann and Bob were dozing and relaxing together on the deck couch. Both knew their relationship was going to work.

Hiking Strawberry Mountain was on their agenda for the following day.

Bob ended the evening. "I don't want to let go. But if I don't leave, I'll be snoring. It feels good to hold you, and I want to continue."

Ann smiled. "I like our direction. No pressure. I've thought about what it might look like living together, like Jim and Jo."

The two stood, and Bob placed an arm around Ann. "I don't know, maybe I'm a stick-in-the-mud, and maybe an old- traditional fart, but I'd like commitment."

"We've got time." Ann kissed Bob goodnight and walked with him to the Jeep. After Bob left, she tidied up and prepared for bed. Chopper was fast asleep in her bed.

27 ENERGY SWIRLS

After opening a window, Ann got into bed. She welcomed the cool breeze that blew through her bedroom. She pulled the cover around her chin. As she drifted off to sleep, she thought of energy swirls and parallel universes. Sometime in the night, she reached for the pad of paper and pencil beside her bed, and she wrote about Eve. More than a dream, she thought, it's like automatic writing while half asleep. The following afternoon, she remembered, and she found the pad in her bedroom. She picked it up and began reading her scribbled writing:

> *The journey is what you make it. My journey was not a bad one. Actually, it was quite good after I got the rhythm. If you eat the juicy apple of separation and come to earth, enjoy it. Don't deny it. It has God seeds to uncover. The joys of loving other humans, of children, of*

painting, of sculpting and eating great food are wonderful. And each contains a God seed. The God seed is the Oneness, the Absolute without limitation. It has no beginning and no end. Unnecessary pain and suffering are caused when one doesn't choose God first, but instead stands in judgment, perceives with ego, takes responsibility for another or hates self. All paths lead to God, but the most direct is to choose God first; find the God seed.

There is the union of the feminine and the masculine within each person, and the sacred and mysterious union of the human with the divine. All is well. All is well. Some use a co-dependence on Jesus and God to separate themselves as being better than others. The message of Jesus is not crucify, crucify. It's resurrect, resurrect. Choose God, or not. It's up to you.

28 AUTHOR'S FINAL THOUGHTS

At one time, I thought the Second Coming of Christ might be in a female body, and that She, too, would be crucified. It would not be on a cross, but rather the feminine within each human would be crucified so that the feminine, as a whole, could resurrect. The feminine and masculine in union were crucified the first time with the body of Christ. The sacred union is the human with the Divine. And Jesus led the way. The crucifixion already occurred. It is finished. It is finished. We are all in union.

We are each whole. The wholeness, the resurrection, leads to the absolute. Perhaps the apple is being in a human body. One, as in a Monopoly game, can go "straight to absolute." Then again, if I picked an apple that took me out of the absolute, I may as well enjoy it. If I were to write a book on the absolute, there would be no words, thoughts, tears or emotions, just empty pages. There is no beginning or end in the absolute. With the absolute, you know the journey and stay in the absolute. One just stays in Eden, with awareness, knowing all is well. No need for emotion, feeling or separation. Heaven is the absolute. So, while I am here in human form, I'm going to enjoy the apples, knowing they expand awareness of God and lead me, or return me, to Eden. There, expansion is inherent in the absolute. May I choose wisely. No wanting for apples in the absolute.

The breath of life is in each of us. I love the cast of characters in the Bible and the old Catholic ritual, but not the continuing patriarchal hierarchy. Something beautiful exists about the mystery of Catholicism and the sacrament of Holy Communion. Would that we all might become one with Christ, instead of creating Christ in our personal image.

Oneness prevails. It is my belief that, where oneness doesn't exist, a door will open for resurrection, thus expanding awareness and returning us to wholeness. Every apple returns me to resurrection and wholeness.

Thank you, Jesus, for having been crucified for all of us.

It is finished!

29 THOUGHTS THAT STARTED ME ON THE JOURNEY

Adam was created by God, but was not his son. Eve was created by God from the rib of Adam. Both Adam and Eve were not natural births, as we recognize birth today. Neither is his only begotten. Eve was created to bring companionship to Adam. Out of that companionship came the eating of the apple, and a population of natural births appears to have begun. Thus began my journey, with my perception of the spirit of Eve.

As a woman, I first began contemplating Eve. And I felt an overwhelming sense of her being the first woman and, of course, Adam the first man. Many times in life, being the first at anything can be a challenge. But to be the first woman! What was it like for her to see the first man? Neither Adam nor Eve had a human mother or father. Here was another being, not exactly the same, but both human. So, who were her mother and father? Yes, I know, she was taken from Adam's rib. But who were his father and mother? Or was it simply a snap of energy, and he breathed?

I saw an icon of Eve, Mother Eve, at a Tudor Paul Scripor workshop at Trinity Cathedral in Phoenix. I was drawn to it like a magnet. Poor excuse, but not having an extra $300 prevented my purchase of it. However, he did allow me to take a photo and paint it. It wasn't until later that I learned most people are afraid of it. The curator of the exhibit said people call it scary. As she said "scary," it was the first time the thought of scary entered my mind as a description of the beautiful glass icon of Mother Eve. In Jungian terms, I would call her a Crone, and even now words such as "Hag" and "Lilith" come to mind as descriptions of the icon, the old woman. I am still not clear whether she's considered a saint; I think not. So, icon would be an inappropriate description. "Portrait," or "sacred portrait," would be better descriptions. I thought Mother Eve had strength and wisdom. Strength and wisdom don't frighten me. She spoke to me.

During a meal with a friend, I mentioned that I might be writing about and painting Eve. Her reaction was, "I'll bet she's beautiful!" Of course, and she is old. How come one of the few times a woman is empowered to make a decision, she was in the Garden of Eden, and she made what appears to be the wrong decision? It wouldn't be the first time a woman was blamed. Both made a decision, even if one of the decisions was to not make a decision. Then, with Cain and Able, the first family existed. The first births were Cain and Able. And what if neither Adam nor Eve had eaten the forbidden fruit? Would none of us have been born as humans on earth? Is that good or bad? Does human birth come from mistake? Fertility appears to begin with biting an apple. Would the cycle of birthing children be nonexistent if they had not eaten the apple? Perhaps there's a relationship between "suffer the little children" and birthing children, as we know both relate to separation. Because we are embryonic, we think we are separate, and original sin began. If not Eve and/or Adam, then another would have been tempted. The snake would morph and appear in many forms of temptation.

In the garden, pre-apple eating, there was a commitment that Adam and Eve made to God to not eat from the tree of knowledge of good and evil. Commitment, to me, means "all" without exception. Yet prenuptials exist, and they mean "not all of me." Adam and Eve, in a way, did a "not all of me." God is the creator of All, including the "not all of me." And within the creation of ALL are the seeds.

Did I mention that Mother Eve is holding a pomegranate filled with seeds? And that in Latin pomegranate means seedy apple? Out of the core of an apple are seeds for several trees and much fruit to continue the apple of choice.

Where are Adam and Eve today? On the other side Re-incarnated or evolved into something else? With God as angels? Did either learn forgiveness or even have a clue as to its meaning? The two of them were the first apple seed.

Eve is, or was, the eternal scapegoat. The beginning of fertility began with both of them; eternally connected. We are all in communion. Eve was the first to be accused of saying "yes" to temptation. An old 60s song comes to mind. The words are, I believe, "we're on the eve of destruction," and, by the grace of God, we make it. Amen.

BIBLIOGRAPY

Man and his Symbols/Carl J. Jung/Aldus Books limited/
London/1964

The Black Madonna/Malgorzata Oleszkiewicz-Peralba/
University of New Mexico Press/New Mexico/2007

The Divine Milieu/Teilhard De Chardin/Harper and
Row/1960

The Phenomenon of Man/Teilhard De Chardin/Harper
and Row/New York/1959

Miracles Every Day: The Story of One Physician's
Inspiring Faith and the Healing Power of Prayer/Maura
Zagrans/ Doubleday Religion, Crown Publishing Group,
Random House, Inc./New York/2010

The Astonishing Power of Emotions/Esther and Jerry
Hicks/Hay House Inc./Carlsbad, California/2007

ABOUT THE AUTHOR

Novelist Nancy Lee Burns is the author of Retirement: Sacred or Scared. She resides in Phoenix, Arizona, and enjoys summers hiking, writing and painting in the mountain village of Pine, Arizona.

You can find her at her Amazon Author Page or email her at nlburns100@yahoo.com